New Testament Church Life, A Model for Today

Charles W. Davis

SECOND PRINTING

BRENTWOOD CHRISTIAN PRESS
COLUMBUS, GEORGIA

New Testament
Church Life,
A Model for Today

To My Wife, Frances,
who has lived the character and spirit
of Jesus before me for more than fifty years

TABLE OF CONTENTS

PART ONE

The New Testament Church

PART TWO

New Testament Church Practices

PART THREE

Leaders of the Church

PART FOUR

The Church Yesterday and Today

FOREWORD

Fifty-three thousand people a week are leaving the church in North America. They are not leaving because they are losing their faith, but to save their faith. Program based, building oriented, platform driven churches are quickly losing their appeal, and rightly so. Followers of Jesus Christ who are serious about their faith are tired of sitting next to strangers for an hour on Sunday mornings, listening to another stranger talk to them. They want something more. And they deserve more. *New Testament Church Life, A Model for Today* describes what people are searching for, without hype, in a stunningly simple manner. Don't miss the message. This book is unvarnished truth.

Most writers writing about New Testament church life assume too much. Charles Davis doesn't make that mistake. He carefully lays a foundation in *New Testament Church Life, A Model for Today* that is essential if we are to understand and follow God's purposes and plans for the church. He builds one truth upon another, chapter by chapter, creating an overview of what church is and how it functions. I kept thinking as I read the manuscript that I had to get this book into the hands of emerging church leaders and church planters I know all over the world.

If you are looking for a "how to grow a church in ten easy steps" type book, this book is not for you. But if you want to discover in one single volume a working definition of church, how it functions, its leadership, church discipline, basic doctrine, in short, all the essentials for planting New Testament churches and laying biblical foundations for existing churches, this is it. I have at least twenty books about church in my library. This book by far gives the most complete, biblical picture of church as God intends it.

Dr. Davis does not make the mistake of advocating a particular model of church. Nor does he write from a Western point of view. He understands the need to grow churches that fit the culture of the people. What he does do is write as a practitioner, one who has traveled the world and pastored for many years. His style is easy to follow; yet he writes with a wealth of biblical scholarship.

I commend this book with heartfelt thanks to Charles Davis. He has been a father and friend to emerging leaders all over the world. His level headed spirituality, his love for God's Word, his years of experience, and his Christ-likeness have inspired all those who know him to live a God fearing life of effective service in God's kingdom and to build the church as co-workers with the Master Builder himself.

Floyd McClung
All Nations
www.floydandsally.com

ACKNOWLEDGMENTS

During almost sixty years in ministry, I have heard an untold number of lectures and sermons and read hundreds of books. I have done my best to acknowledge the sources for the material in this book, but I'm sure that there are those not properly credited. For this I apologize.

I am indebted to my godly parents, to the members of the churches I have served, the students I have taught and colleagues in ministry who have enriched and expanded my life. I am thankful to the leadership team of Antioch Ministries International for allowing me the time and opportunity to write this book. I am especially grateful to Kevin Johnson, who first encouraged me to write it, and to Eugene Morgan, who reduced to writing the videos of my class lectures on New Testament Church Life. I want to express my deepest gratitude to my "faith partners" for their faithful prayer and financial support. My wife, Frances, literally made the book possible by her infinite patience with me during the project and by typing the first draft and many revisions of the manuscript. She has given me unwavering support from start to finish, not the least of which are her prayers.

Words are inadequate to express gratitude to my editor, Pacheco Pyle. She is God's "grace gift" to us. She is thoroughly professional and at the same time a warmhearted, deeply devoted follower of Jesus. Bill, Pacheco's husband, has given much assistance and encouragement.

Most of all, I am inexpressibly grateful to the Lord Jesus Christ through whom "I became a servant of this gospel by the gift of God's grace given me through the working of his power."

PREFACE

This is not a scholarly treatise. An in-depth consideration of the New Testament church requires the writer to place it in its cultural, social, political, economic and religious context, with special emphasis on its Old Testament roots. These factors are essential to a comprehensive understanding of the New Testament and should be considered by every serious student. However, the scope of this book is much more limited. Here we are looking only at what can be seen from the New Testament writings.

The primary purpose is to present a view of a New Testament church that can be replicated in any culture, at any time, at any place in the world, by new or mature Christians. No reference is made to the ongoing debatable theological issues, *i.e.* the nature of Baptism and the Lord's Supper, Calvinism, Armenianism, the role of women in the church, openness theology or similar issues.

There are instances when I used the masculine third person pronoun to include both men and women. I found it awkward to use his/her or she/he on every occasion.

Also, in most cases, when I included English letters for Greek words, I used the present infinitive in order to make it easier for the reader's additional research.

In this book I have cited verses and passages from several translations of the Bible. A list of those used, along with their abbreviations, follows this preface.

Unless otherwise noted, Scripture quotations are from the *New International Version.* Copyright 1973, 1978, 1984, International Bible Society.

Charles W. Davis
Northport, Alabama
2005

BIBLE TRANSLATIONS USED AND THEIR ABBREVIATIONS

AMP   *The Amplified Bible*
         Grand Rapids: Zondervan (1987)

KJV   *King James Version*

NASB   *New American Standard Bible*
         Anaheim, CA: Foundation Press (1973)

NIV   *New International Version*
         Colorado Springs: International Bible Society
         (1984)

NLT   *New Living Translation*
         Wheaton, IL: Tyndale House Publishers (1996)

NRSV   *New Revised Standard Version*
         Grand Rapids: Zondervan (1989, 1990)

Phillips *New Testament in Modern English* by J. B. Phillips
         New York: Macmillan (1958)

RSV   *Revised Standard Version*
         National Council of the Churches of Christ in the
         USA
         Copyright 1971, 1973

Williams *The New Testament* by Charles B. Williams
         Chicago: Moody Press (1960)

PART ONE

The New Testament Church

Chapter One: Orientation

Chapter Two: Basis

Chapter Three: Scope, Metaphors and Pattern

PART ONE
THE NEW TESTAMENT CHURCH

CHAPTER 1

ORIENTATION

Before considering life in the New Testament Church, I need to give some orientation by discussing two subjects:
1. How we know what we know
2. A biblical worldview

HOW WE KNOW WHAT WE KNOW

Epistemology, a division of philosophy, seeks to answer the question, "How do we know what we know?" Generally, epistemology concludes that our knowledge comes by way of reason, intuition and experience. For the Christian there is a fourth way of knowing: revelation.

Knowing God

Everything humans know about God is by his self-disclosure. Unless God tells us about himself, we cannot know him.

Mankind got off on the wrong foot. Adam and Eve chose a creaturely alternative to knowledge in an effort to be independent of God. Echoing Adam and Eve's choice, philosophers throughout history from Aristotle to the present have maintained that God can be discovered through reason alone, a complete contradiction to Scripture.

"For practical purposes, God's self-revelation is found in the Bible, which speaks supremely of the person and work of Jesus Christ, the Word of God incarnate. If something is not corroborated by the Bible, or is contradictory to it, it cannot be regarded as a true statement about God."[1]

I can acquire some knowledge about another person by research and inquiry. But ultimately the in-depth knowledge I have of the "real" person comes from the person's self-disclosure. This is true of all interpersonal relationships and certainly applies to man's relationship with God.

I see people on television talk shows and I think, "How do they come up with some of their conclusions about life?" Then I remember that they don't walk in the revelation of God, but only in the three creaturely means of acquiring knowledge: reason, intuition and experience.

Obedience

The Scripture clearly says that knowledge alone puffs up (I Corinthians 8:1). It inevitably leads to pride and self-sufficiency. Yet Christians are not the *know-nothing* party. Indeed, serious believers pursue knowledge through every means possible, but revelation from God comes through Scripture and obedience to Scripture.

There was a time when I thought that knowledge produced obedience. I taught and taught the Scriptures but didn't see much change in my students.

Then I encountered a teacher younger than my youngest son. At the time, I was a student in a Crossroads Discipleship Training School run by Youth With A Mission (YWAM), and our teacher's knowledge and insight astounded me. Because I had been in ministry longer than he had lived, I wondered, "How could he know so much about God and his ways?"

Before his time with our class was over, I learned that this teacher's authority was based on a lifestyle of unquestioning obedience in every area of his life. His life reflected the words of Jesus, "Those who obey my commandments are the ones who love me. And because they love me, my Father will love them, and I will love them. And I will reveal myself to each one of them" (John 14:21 NLT).

It is evident in this verse that obedience also produces an intimate relationship with God, which should be the desire of every Christian.

Further, obedience results in peace of mind and heart. As Jesus discussed love and obedience in John 14, he said "I am leaving you with a gift—peace of mind and heart. And the peace I give isn't like the peace the world gives. So don't be troubled or afraid" (John 14:27 NLT). Years ago a man working in the refugee camps in Thailand took a time of rest in Bangkok. When asked if he had seen anyone come to faith in the Lord during the two years of his service, he said, "No."

"Then how can you be so radiant and full of joy, when you've seen no results?"

The worker took a while to think, then said, "I guess it's obedience."

Obedience is not a sentiment; it is an action. "...a woman in the crowd called out, 'Blessed is the mother who gave you birth and nursed you.' He replied, 'Blessed rather are those who hear the word of God and obey it'" (Luke 11:27-28).

"The golden rule to follow to obtain spiritual understanding is not one of intellectual pursuit, but one of obedience. If a person wants scientific knowledge, then intellectual curiosity must be his guide. But if he desires knowledge and insight into the teachings of Jesus Christ, he can only obtain it through obedience... "[2]

Obedience to scriptural commands may not produce peaceful circumstances. There is a false teaching that says, "the higher the commitment to God, the higher the comfort level." It simply is not so. Jesus is our example. "Although he was a son, he learned obedience from what he suffered" (Hebrews 5:8). Before his incarnation he owed obedience to no one. He knew what obedience was but had never experienced it until he came in the flesh. He did not move from disobedience to obedience. He learned obedience by obeying. Jesus' obedience was the constant choosing the will of the Father. May God help us to follow his example.

Disobedience

Disobedience prevents receiving revelation from God. Romans 1:21-28 gives details on what disobedience prevents:

Disobedience prevents recognition of God's authority.

(21) "For although they knew God, they neither glorified him as God nor gave thanks to him, but their thinking became futile and their foolish hearts were darkened. (22) Although they claimed to be wise, they became fools (23) and exchanged the glory of the immortal God for images made to look like mortal man and birds and animals and reptiles."

Disobedience prevents distinguishing between Creator and creature.

(24) "Therefore God gave them over in the sinful desires of their hearts to sexual impurity for the degrading of their bodies with one another. (25) They exchanged the truth of God for a lie, and worshiped and served created things rather than the Creator – who is forever praised. Amen."

Disobedience prevents distinguishing between proper sexual roles.

(26) "Because of this, God gave them over to shameful lusts. Even their women exchanged natural relations for unnatural ones. (27) In the same way the men also abandoned natural relations with women and were inflamed with lust for one another. Men committed indecent acts with other men, and received in themselves the due penalty for their perversion."

Disobedience prevents distinguishing between good and evil.

(28) "Furthermore, since they did not think it worthwhile to retain the knowledge of God, he gave them over to a depraved mind, to do what ought not to be done."

No recognition of God's authority, no capacity to distinguish between Creator and creature, no capacity to distinguish between male and female, no capacity to distinguish between good and evil. How do these tragedies come about? Through disobedience to God. A sobering truth.

Long ago Isaiah gave a solemn warning:

"Woe to those who call evil good and good evil, who put darkness for light and light for darkness, who put bitter for sweet and sweet for bitter. Woe to those who are wise in their own eyes and clever in their own sight" (Isaiah 5:20-21).

BIBLICAL WORLDVIEW

An authentic biblical worldview holds that there is a biblical perspective on everything – not just on spiritual matters. Only such a worldview answers the fundamental questions of life: Where did we come from? Who are we? What is the purpose of life? Analysis of any other worldview will reveal its inadequacy to answer such questions. Surprisingly, liberal theologians do not "do theology" based on a biblical worldview. The evidence for this is the rejection of the supernatural and the claim that God works only through natural processes.

The biblical worldview contrasts dramatically with the worldview that prevails in much of contemporary culture. That view holds, among other things, that there is no deity outside the universe, *i.e.*, that reality is one unitary organic whole: "God is all and all is God." New Age and many non-biblical religions hold this view. It is technically known as monism and is diametrically opposed to the biblical belief of monotheism. "...the Lord our God, the Lord is one" (Mark 12:29).

God the Creator

A biblical worldview asserts that God exists apart from the created universe. He is a person. He created everything, seen and unseen. The universe did not cause itself.

Throughout the Old Testament, the motivation for obedience to God was not just that he was the Deliverer, but that he was Creator.

"... Is he not your Father, your Creator, who made you and formed you?" (Deuteronomy 32:6). See also Psalm 33:6-9, Psalm 148:5-6.

Genesis chapter one tells us that a good God created a good world with good people in it. Genesis 1:31 declares, "God saw all that he had made, and it was very good." This was God's assessment of the world he had made.

Any thinking person, observing current world conditions, will ask, "What in the world went wrong? If God is a good God, why is there evil in the world?"

The following offers at least a partial response to this question.

Man the Creature

God made man in his own image (Genesis1:26-27), not similar in appearance or omnipotence, but in personhood. God is a person and he gave man the personal qualities of

1. Mind/Intellect
2. Will/Volition
3. Emotions/Feelings.

The biblical belief that each person is created in the image of God, and therefore of immeasurable worth, is a unique concept among the religions of the world.

As a part of his creative process, God gave something to man that he has never withdrawn – the power of choice. He knew that if our relationship to him was to have any meaning at all, it had to be voluntary. Valid choice requires options. God gave man the option of loving and obeying him or rejecting and disobeying him. He did not make puppets or toys, but persons.

In the account of creation the Bible says that God created mankind "male and female" (Genesis 1:27). For years I struggled with my sexual identity because I appreciated so many things that females appreciated. In a doctor's waiting room, for example, if I had a choice between a magazine on hunting and fishing and another on home interior design, I always selected the latter. Even though I was not sexually attracted to men, I wondered if there were some kind of latent homosexuality in me. Then the truth broke into my spirit, "God created me male and that settles it." The issue never arose in my life again. I knew without a doubt that God created male and female.

The Creation

God not only created mankind; he created heaven and earth for mankind's environment. His creation was *ex nihilo* (from nothing).

"By the word of the Lord were the heavens made, their starry host by the breath of his mouth... For he spoke, and it came to be; he commanded, and it stood firm" (Psalm 33:6-9).

"By faith we understand that the universe was formed at God's command, so that what is seen was not made out of what was visible" (Hebrews 11:3).

"In the beginning He spoke to nothing, and it became *something*. Chaos heard it and became order, darkness heard it and became light. 'And God said – and it was so.' These twin phrases, as cause and effect, occur throughout the Genesis story of the creation. The *said* accounts for the *so*. The *so* is the *said* put into the continuous present."[3]

Responsibility for Creation Care

In Genesis 2:15 we read, "The Lord God took the man and put him in the Garden of Eden to work it and take care of it." The phrase "take care of" may also be translated, "keep watch and protect." We have a biblical responsibility of environmental stewardship. Every Christian should be committed to "creation care."

Nancy Pearcey expands the understanding of the command in Genesis 1:28 to mean far more than care for the physical world. "In Genesis, God gives what we might call the first job description: 'Be fruitful and multiply,' means to develop the social world: build families, churches, schools, cities, governments, laws. The second phrase, 'subdue the earth,' means to harness the natural world: plant crops, build bridges, design computers, compose music. This passage is sometimes called the Cultural Mandate because it tells us that our original purpose was to create cultures, build civilizations – nothing less."[4]

Man the Sinner

With Adam and Eve's choice to disobey God evil entered the human race and continues to this day. "It is perfectly true that in making man as he did God made the possibility of evil. But the bare possibility of evil is not the actualizing of it. And in making that possibility, God validated choice and validated man as man —a being significant in history. If he had left him without choice, you could speak forever of man being man, man being significant, but it would be only meaningless words. All love...is bound up with choice. Without choice the word 'love' is meaningless."[5] "A good God has determined that free will is more valuable than absence of evil... Humanity's present condition is the natural and logical consequence of man's sinful acts... God is not only loving, all-powerful, and just; He is also wise. God's wisdom has made a way for man, in man's own free will, to choose a way out of the bondage and suffering of the world and into relationship with Him. God's powerful, loving, just, and wise solution was Jesus and the Cross (John 3:16)."[6]

When sin entered, it touched everything and everybody. We see it even in the physical world. Before sin there was no single defective cell in any human or animal, no tornadoes or devastating floods or earthquakes. Romans 8:20-22 states that all of creation longs for the perfection it once knew. A natural disaster such as a hurricane or a volcanic eruption is wrongly termed "an act of God." Creation was the act of God, but disasters occur because sin came into the world.

God's Goodness

Though man's sin brought suffering and trouble, God's provision through Jesus Christ will someday liberate all of creation from bondage.

The psalmist said to God in Psalm 119:68, "You are good, and what you do is good... " This conviction will keep us steady even in times of shock and suffering.

My Wife's Assurance of God's Goodness

On a hot afternoon in July, 1985, my wife, Frances, and I were standing in front of our house with a landscaper, discussing the replacement of some dead shrubbery in our yard. Once we had reached an agreement, Frances went to retrieve her purse from the trunk of our car, which was parked at the curb in front of our house. As I continued to talk with the landscaper, I heard a loud crash. To my horror, I turned to see that a car had rolled quickly down the steep hill nearby, crashing into the back of our car.

Panic stricken, I ran to the street, calling Frances' name because I couldn't see where she was. Then I saw her pinned between the two cars, her left leg crushed. Fortunately, one wheel of the rolling car had hit the curb, weakening the impact, or both her legs would have been crushed.

While we waited for the ambulance to arrive, I leaned toward the trunk where she lay crumpled and tried to console her. "Sweetie, hold on," I said. "The emergency people will be here soon".

Her first response to me was, "Let's stand on Romans 8:28, 'And we know that in all things God works for the good of those who love him, who have been called according to his purpose.'" In surgery, the doctors worked for several hours to save Frances' leg. Later when she lay in the Intensive Care Unit, I spoke with her again. Despite strong medication, she was still in severe pain. Knowing that she had been in and out of consciousness, I asked Frances if she remembered what she said to me while she was pinned between the cars. She answered, "Yes, I do. And I want to declare that I love the Lord and I love his ways."

A person doesn't settle this issue at the time of a crisis. It must be settled earlier when you get it fixed forever in your heart that God is a good God and all he does is good.

We later learned that a girl had received a new car for her sixteenth birthday; and in her haste to show it to a friend, she had parked the car on the hill without securing it. Silently it had rolled down the hill and crushed my wife's leg.

During 18 months of rehabilitation and two additional surgeries, Frances did not waver from her settled position of trusting God. Unfortunately, a setback occurred during one surgery when the doctor accidentally broke her leg again as he tried to increase the angle of the bend of her knee. The new break meant that she had to make a new beginning in her healing and rehab. As a result of that operating room accident, she walks with a stiff leg.

Even with this disability and frequent pain, she has traveled with me to many parts of the world, ministering especially to women. God has used her testimony to encourage others and to bring glory to himself.

My Own Test of Confidence in the Goodness of God

In October of 1996, while driving to Richmond, Virginia, to teach in a Youth With A Mission (YWAM) Church Planting and Leadership School, I felt severe pain throughout my body and also felt feverish. At our destination for that night, my wife and I checked in a motel and discovered that my temperature was 102 degrees.

The next day we drove on to Richmond. My temperature had dropped, but I still had severe pain throughout my body. The following day I began teaching in the school.

That night I woke up drenched in perspiration and had to change my pajamas. The next morning I called my doctor, and she insisted that I return to Alabama and check in to the hospital immediately. I was distressed at her insistence because it meant I would not complete the teaching assignment, but I complied with her demand.

After a five-day stay in the hospital, I received the news from a team of specialists who had determined that I had Polymyalgia Rheumatica (PMR), an inflammation throughout the body, including arteries, ligaments, tendons and bones.

If the temple arteries become inflamed they can cause blindness, so after leaving the first hospital I was admitted to another for a biopsy of the temple arteries.

Besides the concern about my health and the discomfort, I struggled with fear and dread about the very future of my ministry. I was grateful when the biopsy proved negative, but I knew that all was not well.

Pervasive pain, lack of appetite, loss of energy, fatigue and depression assailed me. This difficult time was even worse for my wife and me because my ministry was "on hold."

Eventually, medication eliminated most of the symptoms – except for the pain, which persists at varying levels to this very day.

I praise God that after a few months I was able to resume my ministry, despite pain that at times has been almost disabling. But God has been completely faithful to sustain me through it. Because of the precious truths I learned about God, I can say with the Psalmist, "It was good for me to be afflicted so that I might learn your decrees" (Psalm 119:71).

These and other difficult life experiences have not diminished my complete conviction that God is a good God and what He does is good.

How's Your Shirt Buttoned?

As everyone knows, if you button the first button on your shirt wrong, all the other buttons will be buttoned wrong. Some things need to get settled up front. The first "button" is to know the character of God. If that issue isn't correct, you'll struggle with button four or five and cry out, "Why, God?"

I've always been a fragile person, physically and emotionally. My mother said it began with prolonged colic as a baby. My earliest childhood memories are of visits to the doctor's office with stomach problems. At age 12, I had surgery to correct chronic sinusitis. At age 15 I had rheumatic fever, which at that time was treated with extended bed rest. Once I was allowed to get up, I could barely walk, and the rehabilitation was painful and lengthy. I had pneumonia during two winters of my high school years.

In addition to the physical challenges, I have experienced a number of bouts with clinical depression.

I've asked God to make me physically and emotionally strong. I've prayed and sought the prayers of many godly people. God has chosen not to fully heal me. All I can do is give who I am, how I am, to God. When I do that, he'll use me.

It's not ability; it's availability. We must not wait until we have everything together. We can trust a good God to always act in our best interest, whatever circumstance we are in.

"For the Lord is good and his love endures forever;
his faithfulness continues through all generations"
(Psalm 100:5).

I am Exhibit A that God can use common clay pots – earthen vessels. (II Corinthians 4:7)

> "My grace is sufficient for you, for my power is made perfect in weakness… For when I am weak, then I am strong" (II Corinthians 12:9-10).

That is my testimony.

All of creation has been touched, distorted and twisted by sin. For those of us who know God, the grace of God pours in during times of pain and suffering. Some say, "Why me?" But why not me? We *all* live in this broken world. Some of us want to believe we're living in heaven now in every way, but as Elizabeth Elliott says, "Heaven is not here; it's there."

Satan: Accuser, Murderer and Liar

Satan is real; he is a personal devil. He is not God nor equal with God. He's a created and limited being. His names indicate who he is. In Greek the word *devil* means accuser or slanderer.

Jesus described him:

> "… He was a murderer from the beginning, not holding to the truth, for there is no truth in him. When he lies, he speaks his native language, for he is a liar and the father of lies" (John 8:44).

Jesus assured us:

> "Then you will know the truth, and the truth will set you free" (John 8:32).

Jesus prayed for us.

> "My prayer is not that you take them out of the world but that you protect them from the evil one… Sanctify them by the truth; your word is truth" (John 17:15, 17).

"Since Satan's primary weapon is the lie, your defense against him is the truth. Dealing with Satan is not a power encounter; it's a truth encounter. When you expose Satan's lie with God's truth, his power is broken... Satan's lie cannot withstand the truth any more than the darkness of night can withstand the light of the rising sun."[7]

The first piece of spiritual armor mentioned in Ephesians 6 is truth:

> "Stand firm then, with the belt of truth buckled around your waist... " (Ephesians 6:14).

The only power Satan has over the Christian is the power of deception. His method is persuasive lies. His big lie is that God cannot be trusted. He started this with Eve (Genesis 3:1).

Satan: Defeated Adversary

Satan means adversary, but he is a *defeated* adversary. Jesus said,

> "Now is the time for judgment on this world; now the prince of this world will be driven out" (John 12:31).

John said,

> "... The reason the Son of God appeared was to destroy the devil's work" (1 John 3:8). See also Colossians 2:13-15.

I'm aware of the devil but I'm not afraid of him. God has provided adequate armor for his defeat (Ephesians 6:10-20). This Ephesians passage deserves in-depth and repeated study.

The Primacy of the Bible

Implicit in holding a biblical worldview is the belief in the primacy of Scripture over tradition, reason and experience. Richard Hays states it well: "Scripture is not just one among several 'classics,' not just one source of moral wisdom competing in a marketplace of ideas, experiences, and feelings. Scripture is the wellspring of life, the fundamental source for the identity of the church."[8]

The Beeson Divinity School doctrinal statement reflects this conviction: "God has once and for all revealed Himself to us through the words of Holy Scripture which we believe to have 'God for its author, salvation for its end, and truth without any mixture of error for its matter.' The Bible is the supreme standard by which all human conduct and opinion should be tried."[9]

To assume the primacy of the Bible is to believe that there is objective, absolute truth; there is a universal standard of right and wrong that applies to all cultures. The pervasive attitude of today argues that there is no absolute truth. There is only each individual's, or each group's, perspective on the truth; and all perspectives are equally valid. This philosophy of postmodernism places mankind on the slippery slope toward the disintegration of society. A Christian, biblical worldview depends on the absolute truth claims of Scripture.

This chapter has presented an essential orientation to understanding my approach to New Testament church life.

CHAPTER 2

THE BASIS

DEFINITION: A New Testament church is a group of baptized believers, of any number, committed to proclaiming and living out the Gospel of Jesus Christ under his lordship.

As the Good News of Christ reached the people of the Roman World, those who believed the message began to meet together in small groups and in the temple courts. The basis of their church life was

The Incarnation
The Cross
The Resurrection
The Coming of the Holy Spirit

THE INCARNATION
Old Testament Prophecies

The coming of Christ as the Messiah was predicted by the Old Testament prophets.

Seven hundred years before the birth of Christ, the prophet Isaiah declared,

"Therefore the Lord himself will give you a sign: The virgin will be with child and will give birth to a son, and will call him Immanuel" (Isaiah 7:14).

Matthew confirmed the fulfillment of this prophecy by quoting Isaiah,

"'The virgin will be with child and will give birth to a son, and they will call him Immanuel: – which means 'God with us.'" (Matthew 1:23).

The prophet Micah predicted the place of Christ's birth.

"But you, Bethlehem Ephrathah, though you are small among the clans of Judah, out of you will come for me one who will be ruler over Israel, whose origins are from of old, from ancient times" (Micah 5:2).

Isaiah prophesied the way Christ would die.

"But he was pierced for our transgressions, he was crushed for our iniquities; the punishment that brought us peace was upon him, and by his wounds we are healed" (Isaiah 53:5).

Approximately 35 prophetic passages in the Old Testament refer to Christ and are fulfilled in the New Testament. The mathematical probability of any three being fulfilled randomly is ten to the fifteenth power, a number most of us cannot comprehend.

Incarnation in the New Testament

The word *incarnation* is not found in the New Testament but the words "in flesh" are frequently used to describe the coming of God's Son to earth in human form. The hymn quoted in I Timothy 3:16 declares, "... He was revealed in flesh" (NRSV). Paul said that Christ did his reconciling work in his physical body (literally, "in his body of flesh," Colossians 1:22, RSV). Peter wrote of Christ dying for us "in the flesh" (Greek: *sarki*) in I Peter 3:18 (RSV).

"The Word became flesh and made his dwelling among us" (John 1:14).

John defined the "Word":

"In the beginning was the Word, and the Word was with God, and the Word was God" (John 1:1).

"The pre-existence of the Word is strongly brought out in the Greek structure... Literally it could and should be rendered 'When the Beginning began, the Word was already there.'"[10]

"The Word was with God." The preposition *with* indicates both equality and distinction, along with association. "And the Word was God" affirms that God, without ceasing to be God, was made man.

"The incarnation of the Son of God, then, was not a diminishing of deity, but an acquiring of manhood. It was not that God the Son came to indwell a human being, as the Spirit was later to do... It was rather that the Son in person began to live a fully human life."[11]

The Lord Jesus Christ lived on the earth as fully God and fully human, a reality beyond our understanding. As such, he is the only qualified mediator between God and man.

"For there is one God and one mediator between God and men, the man Christ Jesus..." (I Timothy 2:5).

The humanity of Christ was a requisite part of the New Testament message.

"This is how you can recognize the Spirit of God. Every spirit that acknowledges that Jesus Christ has come in the flesh is from God, but every spirit that does not acknowledge Jesus is not from God. This is the spirit of the antichrist, which you have heard is coming and even now is already in the world" (I John 4:2-3).

The early Christians enthusiastically announced,

"That which was from the beginning, which we have heard, which we have seen with our eyes, which we have looked at and our hands have touched – this we proclaim concerning the Word of life. The life appeared; we have seen it and testify to it, and we proclaim to you the eternal life, which was with the Father and has appeared to us" (I John 1:1-2).

The writer of the book of Hebrews exclaimed,

"In the past God spoke to our forefathers through the prophets at many times and in various ways, but in these last days he has spoken to us by his Son, whom he appointed heir of all things, and through whom he made the universe. The Son is the radiance of God's glory and the exact representation of his being, sustaining all things by his powerful word. After he had provided purification for sins, he sat down at the right hand of the Majesty in heaven" (Hebrews 1:1-3).

"When God drew aside the curtain of eternity and stepped into human history in the man Jesus, he fully assumed the human condition down to the last joyful or painful experience."[12]

"For we do not have a high priest who is unable to sympathize with our weaknesses, but we have one who has been tempted in every way, just as we are – yet was without sin. Let us then approach the throne of grace with confidence, so that we may receive mercy and find grace to help us in our time of need" (Hebrews 4:15-16).

The doctrine of the incarnation is not some remote theological abstract. It is a precious truth that brings comfort and assurance in every situation of life.

The Apostle Paul made an unrivaled statement of the purpose of the incarnation in his letter to the Philippians:

"Your attitude should be the same as that of Christ Jesus: Who, being in very nature God, did not consider equality with God something to be grasped, but made himself nothing, taking the very nature of a servant, being made in human likeness. And being found in appearance as a man, he humbled himself and became obedient to death – even death on a cross! Therefore God exalted him to the highest place and gave him the name that is above every name, that at the name of Jesus every knee should bow, in heaven and on earth and under the earth, and every tongue confess that Jesus Christ is Lord, to the glory of God the Father" (Philippians 2:5-11).

Hundreds, if not thousands, died on crosses at the hands of the Romans. The cross was the most common method of execution. Without the incarnation, the cross of Christ would have no significance. "Many had died by crucifixion – there were two others on the first Good Friday – and their death laid on mankind no signal blessing. His death has power because it is *his* death."[13]

With full confidence in the scriptural record we can speak the words of the Apostles' Creed:

> I believe in God the Father Almighty,
> Maker of heaven and earth,
> And in Jesus Christ his only Son our Lord;
> Who was conceived by the Holy Spirit,
> Born of the Virgin Mary,
> Suffered under Pontius Pilate,
> Was crucified, dead and buried;
> And descended into Hades.
> The third day he rose again from the dead.
> He ascended into heaven...

The words of Charles Wesley's hymn speak eloquently of the meaning of the incarnation for us as believers:

Come, Thou long-expected Jesus, Born to set Thy people free;
From our fears and sins release us; Let us find our rest in Thee.
Israel's strength and consolation, Hope of all the earth thou art:
Dear Desire of ev'ry nation, Joy of ev'ry longing heart.

Born Thy people to deliver, Born a child, and yet a King,
Born to reign in us forever – Now Thy gracious kingdom bring.
By Thine own eternal Spirit Rule in all our hearts alone;
By Thine all-sufficient merit, Raise us to Thy glorious throne.

THE CROSS

"In Old Greenwich, Connecticut, stands a church with a cross in it... bolted down into the concrete floor in front of the platform... Nothing about this cross is pretty. It is made of raw, untreated wood, and when you see it up close, you think of splinters, of something hard... immovable... There is nothing comfortable about the cross...

"A second cross stands... outside, near the front of the church, clearly visible from the street... When it rains, this cross drips red. Rust red. The concrete under the cross is now permanently stained, and each time it rains, the cement receives a fresh new splattering."[14]

Obviously, that church wants to emphasize the cross as its focus. "The cross is the central event of time and eternity and the answer to all the problems of both."[15] Time and again the Apostle Paul declared the cross of Christ central to the Christian life and the Christian message:

> "May I never boast except in the cross of the Lord Jesus Christ, through which the world has been crucified to me, and I to the world" (Galatians 6:14).

> "But we preach Christ crucified: a stumbling block to the Jews and foolishness to the Gentiles; but to those whom God has called, both Jews and Greeks, Christ, the power of God and the wisdom of God" (I Corinthians 1:23-24).

> "For I resolved to know nothing while I was with you except Jesus Christ and him crucified" (I Corinthians 2:2).

Man's problem was sin – and God dealt with it at the cross because "Sin is a knot that only God can untie."[16]

Romans 3:23 tells us that "all have sinned and fall short of the glory of God." What is sin? Can it be defined only as adultery, drunkenness, and other terrible things? To understand what sin is really like, we need to see how it started with Adam and Eve. Prior to disobeying God, their fellowship with him was good, the way God intended to relate to his creation. He walked with them and talked with them. God's desire was for relationship. But after they chose to disobey God, that relationship was marred and

> "...they hid from the Lord God among the trees of the garden. But the Lord God called to the man, 'Where are you?'" (Genesis 3:8-9).

The basic nature of sin is asserting the right to myself – to be in charge and in control of my own life. Sin is:

Rebellion
Declaring independence from God
Rejecting God's authority
Severing any personal relationship with God
A preoccupation with self and a rejection of God's claim on me.

We cannot fully appreciate the work of the cross until we recognize the gravity of our own sin.

The New Testament uses five Greek words for sin:

hamartia – missing a target; failure to reach a goal
adikia – unrighteousness, iniquity, a deep-seated inward corruption
poneria - degenerate evil, perversion of character
parabasia, paraptoma – a trespass or transgression, the stepping over a known boundary
anomia – lawlessness, disregard or violation of known moral law.

God provided a brilliant and compassionate solution to the sin problem.

> "You see, at just the right time, when we were still powerless, Christ died for the ungodly. Very rarely will anyone die for a righteous man, though for a good man someone might possibly dare to die. But God demonstrates his own love for us in this: While we were still sinners, Christ died for us" (Romans 5:6-8).

> "For all have sinned and fall short of the glory of God, and are justified freely by his grace through the redemp-

tion that came by Christ Jesus. God presented him as a sacrifice of atonement, through faith in his blood. He did this to demonstrate his justice, because in his forbearance he had left the sins committed beforehand unpunished – he did it to demonstrate his justice at the present time, so as to be just and the one who justifies those who have faith in Jesus" (Romans 3:23-26).

Important Words, Important Truths

Justification, redemption, propitiation, reconciliation – big sounding theological words! Yet we find thrilling truth in them concerning the work of the cross.

Justification comes from the courtroom; it's a forensic term, the verdict of a judge. "Justified freely by his grace" (Romans 3:24) means that we're declared *not guilty*. God sees us as innocent as newborn babies without any penalty to pay.

God's grace is demonstrated in that the judge is the one who was himself judged, the one who took our penalty. *Justified* is the opposite of *condemned,* which means tried on the basis of the evidence, convicted on the basis of the evidence, and sentenced to the consequences on the basis of the evidence. All of us, because we're sinners, deserve to be condemned. But God in his grace has declared us *not guilty*. "There is now no condemnation to those who are in Christ Jesus" (Romans 8:1). To be justified means to be pronounced righteous even while we're still sinners.

John Stott puts it this way, "When God justifies sinners, He is not declaring bad people to be good; He is pronouncing them legally righteous, free from any liability to the broken law, because He Himself in His Son has borne the penalty of their law-breaking."[17]

> "What then, shall we say in response to this? If God is for us, who can be against us? He who did not spare his own Son, but gave him up for us all – how will he not also, along with him, graciously give us all things? Who will bring any charge against those whom God has chosen? It is God who justifies. Who is he that condemns? Christ

Jesus, who died – more than that, who was raised to life – is at the right hand of God and is also interceding for us" (Romans 8:31-34).

Grasp the picture here. God is qualified to bring the charge, but he doesn't. He has justified us. Christ Jesus is qualified to condemn, but he doesn't. He died for us and is at the right hand of God making intercession for us!

Continuing in Romans 8, verses 36 and following, assures us that absolutely nothing can separate us from God's love, centered in the cross.

"The essence of sin is man substituting himself for God; the essence of salvation is God substituting Himself for man."[18]

"Justification means this miracle: that Christ takes our place and we take His."[19]

In this, God will not be inconsistent with his own character. He cannot ignore sin and remain righteous and just.

God "...demonstrate(s) his justice at the present time, so as to be just and the one who justifies the man who has faith in Jesus" (Romans 3:26).

In the act of the cross, God can be just and we can be justified. God could have condemned us to die, but where would his love be? He could have excused us, but where would his justice and righteousness be?

The cross of Christ allows God to demonstrate both justice and love. In the cross, God's justice and righteousness joined his love and grace. What a glorious provision, one that only God could have arranged!

"Justification is the great doctrine which is the bedrock of our self-worth. 'Therefore having been justified by faith, we have peace with God through our Lord Jesus Christ' (Romans 5:1)... ' Justification is the judicial act of God by which He declares us free from the guilt of sin... However, as marvelous as that is, justification means more than being forgiven. God not only forgives our sinfulness; He also provides our righteousness... the worthiness to stand in God's presence without the fear of personal condemnation because He has imputed the very righteousness of Christ to us."[20]

Not only do we need to understand justification for ourselves, but we need to be able to communicate it to others. For this reason we must emphasize the cross as a basic doctrine of the New Testament church.

In many evangelism tracts I have read, the suggested prayer for salvation makes no reference to the cross or to sin. This is a grievous omission. In my opinion, an appropriate prayer would be:

> "Lord Jesus, thank you for dying on the cross for my sins. I open the door of my life and trust you as Savior and Lord. Thank you for forgiving me of my sins and giving me eternal life. Take control of the throne of my life. Make me the kind of person you want me to be."

Redemption originally meant the price paid for a slave. An Old Testament example is Hosea who redeemed his wife Gomer, paying six ounces of silver and ten bushels of barley to purchase her from a slave market (Hosea 3:1-3). Jesus paid the price to set us free from slavery to sin. We are no longer under the bondage of sin.

> "For all have sinned and fall short of the glory of God, and are justified freely by his grace through the redemption that came by Christ Jesus" (Romans 3:23-24).

> "It is for freedom that Christ has set us free" (Galatians 5:1).

Jesus gave his life as a ransom, paying the price for our freedom. The Early Church proclaimed the message of Christ's cross.

> "For even the Son of Man did not come to be served, but to serve, and to give his life as a ransom for many" (Mark 10:45).

Propitiation, as rendered in the King James Version, is translated "sacrifice of atonement" in the New International Version (Romans 3:25). This word comes from the language of the temple. On the Old Testament Day of Atonement, the priests offered animals without defect as a sacrifice for the sins of the people. Propitiation means a sacrifice that turns away the anger and wrath of God.

Revelation 13:8 speaks of Jesus as "the Lamb that was slain from the creation of the world."

> "For you know that it was not with perishable things such as silver or gold that you were redeemed from the empty way of life handed down to you from your forefathers, but with the precious blood of Christ, *a lamb without blemish or defect* (italics mine). He was chosen before the creation of the world, but was revealed in these last times for your sake" (I Peter 1:18-20).

Jesus became not only the perfect, but more importantly the *final* sacrifice for sin.

> "He did not enter by means of the blood of goats and calves; but he entered the Most Holy Place once for all by his own blood, having obtained eternal redemption" (Hebrews 9:12).

> "Then Christ would have had to suffer many times since the creation of the world. But now he has appeared once for all at the end of the ages to do away with sin by the *sacrifice* (italics mine) of himself" (Hebrews 9:26).

Our false conception of wrath makes God's wrath an unpopular subject. It is not a divine temper tantrum. John Stott explains, "The wrath of God is His consistent, uncompromising antagonism to evil in all its forms. Just as grace stands for the gracious personal activity of God Himself, wrath stands for His equally personal hostility to evil. God is a holy God; His holiness exposes sin; His wrath opposes it."[21]

Wrath is a logical expression of God's holiness. Our anger, provoked by many things, cannot be compared to God's anger, which is provoked only by evil. Here we see the absolute necessity of the cross. In the cross, God's love found a way to turn his wrath and anger from us and receive it on himself in the person of Jesus Christ. A deeply moving and profound truth.

> "God made him who had no sin to be sin for us, so that in him we might become the righteousness of God" (II Corinthians 5:21).

Sometimes we get the picture that God the Father is angry and punishing the loving Christ, but the loving Father was in Christ reconciling the world to himself. See II Corinthians 5:19.

"In one painting of the Crucifixion the hands of God may be seen, through the darkness that shrouds the cross, supporting the two pierced hands of Jesus, and beyond, the face of God, full of agony."[22]

"God got into it all on Calvary, just so that he could go on being God forever without asking or needing anybody's permission or forgiveness."[23]

The cross shows not only the justice of God but the love of God.

> "This is how we know what love is: Jesus Christ laid down his life for us. And we ought to lay down our lives for our brothers" (I John 3:16).

Apart from Christ and his cross, the world would never have known real love. If you ever wonder whether God loves you or not, just take a look at the cross, the ultimate expression of his love.

> "This is love: not that we loved God, but that he loved us and sent his Son as an atoning sacrifice for our sins" (I John 4:10).

Reconciliation, an intensely personal and intimate family term, means to restore relationship or friendship.

> "Since we have now been justified by his blood, how much more shall we be saved from God's wrath through him! For if, when we were God's enemies, we were reconciled to him through the death of his Son, how much

more, having been reconciled, shall we be saved through his life! Not only is this so, but we also rejoice in God through our Lord Jesus Christ, through whom we have now received reconciliation" (Romans 5:9-11).

"Justification is our legal standing before our judge in the court; reconciliation is our personal relationship with our Father in the home. Two other words 'adoption' and 'access' confirm this emphasis... "[24] To be right with God the judge is a great thing, but to be loved and cared for by God the Father is greater.

"How great is the love the Father has lavished on us, that we should be called children of God! And that is what we are! The reason the world does not know us is that it did not know him. Dear friends, now we are children of God, and what we will be has not yet been made known. But we know that when he appears, we shall be like him, for we shall see him as he is. Everyone who has this hope in him purifies himself, just as he is pure" (I John 3:1-3).

We are children with a loving heavenly Father. Living in this truth, we have a unique viewpoint from which we can see other facets of God's personality and character. Neil Anderson expresses it this way: "Getting right with God always begins with settling once and for all the issue that God is your loving Father and you are his accepted child. That's the foundational truth of your spiritual identity."[25]

Jesus came to reveal the Father. Though the Old Testament has less than a dozen references to God as Father, in the New Testament Jesus referred to God as Father 168 times. For instance, in the Sermon on the Mount Jesus used the term 13 times. When Phillip asked Jesus to show him the Father, Jesus responded,

"Don't you know me, Philip, even after I have been among you such a long time? Anyone who has seen me has seen the Father. How can you say, 'Show us the Father'? Don't you believe that I am in the Father, and that the Father is in me? The words I say to you are not just my own. Rather, it is the Father, living in me, who is doing his work" (John 14:8-10).

The Apostle Paul's writings assume God as Father.

"For you did not receive a spirit that makes you a slave again to fear, but you received the Spirit of sonship. And by him we cry, '*Abba* Father.' The Spirit himself testifies with our spirit that we are God's children. Now if we are children, then we are heirs – heirs of God and co-heirs with Christ, if indeed we share in his sufferings in order that we may also share in his glory" (Romans 8:15-17).

The phrase "*Abba* Father" appears only three times in all Scripture. Jesus used it in Gethsemane, in the deepest crisis of his earthly life.

"Going a little farther, he fell to the ground and prayed that if possible the hour might pass from him. '*Abba*, Father,' he said, 'everything is possible for you. Take this cup from me. Yet not what I will, but what you will'" (Mark 14:35-36).

We have been reconciled to God as Father, so we, like Jesus can come to him and say, "*Abba* Father" in our crisis times.

In New Testament times, little children used *Abba* as an endearing term for father, indicating intimate relationship. We have this privilege with our Father God. When my wife and I were living in Santiago, Chile, we loved to hear the little children next door greet their father when he came home at the end of the day. They ran to him, wrapped their arms around his legs and yelled, "*Popi, Popi!*" in a beautiful illustration of what *Abba* means.

Ephesians 5:1 refers to us as dearly loved children of God with access to the Father. God responds to us because he loves us as a Father.

"The Spirit himself testifies with our spirit that we are God's children" (Romans 8:16). The Greek word *summartureo*, translated "testifies," is in the present tense and indicates continuous action. The Spirit of God constantly tells us that we are God's children. If we don't listen to him, we will have the slavish spirit of fear. The Holy Spirit constantly whispers to us that we're loved by God, *pouring out* the knowledge of God's love for us.

"And hope does not disappoint us, because God has poured out his love into our hearts by the Holy Spirit, whom he has given us" (Romans 5:5).

Poured out symbolizes sowing seeds pervasively. He sows in our hearts a constant knowledge of the Father's love for us, flooding our hearts, assuring us that we are reconciled with God.

"Because you are sons, God sent the Spirit of his Son into our hearts, the Spirit who calls out, '*Abba*, Father.' So you are no longer a slave, but a son; and since you are a son, God has made you also an heir" (Galatians 4:6-7).

Justification, redemption, and propitiation are wonderful truths, but reconciliation touches my heart even more profoundly.

Reconciliation and Our Earthly Fathers

Relating to God as Father can be difficult when looking at him through the grid of an earthly father. For example, one who has experienced his earthly father to be unreliable, will be hesitant to rely on the heavenly Father.

An outstanding, mature missionary woman related that when she was a small child her parents divorced and she lived with her mother. Often her father promised to pick her up and take her to get ice cream. She would sit on the curb of the street, eagerly awaiting him. But he would never show up. She said, "I know it isn't true, but I still feel that when I need my heavenly Father the most, he won't show up."

Ask the Holy Spirit to show you if you have a twisted view of God because if you do, you will live a twisted life. In the hard times Satan will use that distorted view to tell you God is unjust. If you are aware of a charge against God, you can make a choice of your will to drop that charge and begin a new trust in your heavenly Father.

Though the term *Father* is used in Scripture, God's love encompasses every love – a father's love, a mother's love, a sibling's love, even the love of husband or wife. "Our Father's love" does not refer to maleness but to every love that can be known.

Victory

Another aspect of the cross is victory, in all its dimensions.

"When you were dead in your sins and in the uncircumcision of your sinful nature, God made you alive with Christ. He forgave us all our sins, having canceled the written code, with its regulations, that was against us and that stood opposed to us; he took it away, nailing it to the cross. And having disarmed the powers and authorities, he made a public spectacle of them, triumphing over them by the cross" (Colossians 2:13-15).

"A public spectacle" (verse 15) presents the image of a conquering hero leading his captives in a victory procession through the city. Jesus took captive the rulers, authorities, powers and spiritual forces of evil (Ephesians 6:12) and led them in his victory procession.

The language of victory is all through the New Testament:

"...in all these things we are more than conquerors through him who loved us" (Romans 8:37).

"But thanks be to God! He gives us the victory through our Lord Jesus Christ" (I Corinthians 15:57).

"But thanks be to God, who always leads us in triumphal procession in Christ and through us spreads everywhere the fragrance of the knowledge of him" (II Corinthians 2:14).

Paul constantly preached "Christ crucified," the heart of the gospel.

"...I want to remind you of the gospel I preached to you... That Christ died for our sins according to the Scriptures, that he was buried, that he was raised on the third day according to the Scriptures..." (I Corinthians 15:1-4).

The cross leads to Christ's resurrection, the confirmation and demonstration of his complete victory.

Death to Sin

As for applying the victory of the cross to our personal lives,

"What shall we say, then? Shall we go on sinning so that grace may increase? By no means! We died to sin; how can we live in it any longer? Or don't you know that all of us who were baptized into Christ Jesus were baptized into his death? We were therefore buried with him through baptism into death in order that, just as Christ was raised from the dead through the glory of the Father, we too may live a new life. If we have been united with him like this in his death, we will certainly also be united with him in his resurrection. For we know that our old self was crucified with him so that the body of sin might be done away with, that we should no longer be slaves to sin" (Romans 6:1-6).

Our old self was crucified with him, and we are no longer slaves to sin. The cross has given Christians a *legal death* to sin. When we put our faith in Christ, we were baptized into his death – this was an event of the past, establishing a relationship with God that will never change. With Paul, our position in Christ is

"...crucified with Christ and I no longer live, but Christ lives in me. The life I live in the body, I live by faith in the Son of God, who loved me and gave himself for me" (Galatians 2:20).

The response may be, "But Paul was super-spiritual." No, he was talking about all of us.[26]

Death to Self

Another aspect of what the cross means to the believer is **death to self**. While death to sin is an event of the past and an accomplished fact, death to self is daily, deliberately choosing to put to death the old nature. This is the *moral death*. Jesus said,

> "If anyone would come after me, he must deny himself and take up his cross daily and follow me. For whoever wants to save his life will lose it, but whoever loses his life for me will save it" (Luke 9:23-24).

To deny ourselves is to behave toward ourselves as Peter behaved toward Jesus the night of his betrayal. The same Greek word is used both in the case of Jesus' statement in the Luke 9 passage above and in his prediction of Peter's behavior (Luke 22:34, 61). This denial is a daily choice, giving up my right to myself and deciding that I am no longer the center of my world. It is deliberate repudiation and rejection of the selfish life.

Oswald Chambers, in his daily devotional book, *My Utmost For His Highest*, wrote, "The nature of sin is my claim to my right to myself... The nature of sin is not immorality and wrongdoing, but the nature of self-realization which leads us to say, 'I am my own god.' This nature may exhibit itself in proper morality or in improper immorality, but it always has a common basis – my claim to my right to myself."[27]

Denying oneself is not an easy decision, but a deliberate intent and deliberate choice of the will. The cross is not just the entrance to salvation; it is a fundamental element of the Christian life, as indicated by Jesus in the Luke 9 passage quoted above. Like the church in Greenwich, Connecticut, the Christian life must have the cross in the middle of it all the time, not as a morbid, self-inflicted martyr spirit, but as simple biblical reality. No matter what we try to overcome, we are merely dealing with symptoms until we accept the centrality of the cross in our lives.

Paul wrote to the church in Rome,

> "Therefore, brothers, we have an obligation – but it is not to the sinful nature [flesh], to live according to it. For if

you live according to the sinful nature [flesh], you will die; but if by the Spirit you put to death the misdeeds of the body, you will live" (8:12-13).

In this case, *flesh* refers not to the physical body, but to the tendency within each of us to operate independently of God and to center interests and energies on ourselves – the appetites, desires, drives and needs that make for self-gratification and self-pleasing.

C. S. Lewis wrote, "I [Jesus] have not come to torment your natural self but to kill it. No half measures are any good. I don't want to cut off a branch here or a branch there. I want to have the whole tree cut down."[28]

The point is not to do away with our personality or the giftedness God has given us; but, by the power of the cross, to live without surrender to the tyranny of the flesh. "What we are (our self or personal identity) is partly the result of the creation (the image of God) and partly the result of the Fall (the image defaced). The self we are to deny, disown and crucify is our fallen self, everything within us that is incompatible with Jesus Christ."[29]

Death to the World

Another dimension to the cross life is that we are **dead to the world**.

"May I never boast except in the cross of our Lord Jesus Christ, through which the world has been crucified to me, and I to the world" (Galatians 6:14).

In this context *the world* is godless human society, unbelievers thinking and speaking and acting out of their unredeemed nature. The world is collectively or corporately all that the flesh is individually. For example, when a world system like communism operates, it can be more devastating than the individual parts. The world system orders itself against God. The *flesh* is the foothold that the devil has within us. The *world* is the means through which he exerts pressure on us from without. Never forget: you are going to live a life full of pressure. Jesus promised us,

"In this world you will have trouble [pressures]. But take heart! I have overcome the world" (John 16:33).

The word *trouble* means pressures. In Spanish it is *aflicciones*, which is translated into English as afflictions or tribulations or troubles. This is not stoic resignation, but an honest regard for reality.

When I was young, I was idealistic and thought life must be better somewhere else. As I matured, I realized that pressures and troubles are a part of everyone's life. The pressures and troubles are certain; the peace of Jesus is a possibility. Jesus says, "In me you *may* have peace." We have to make the choice. If we choose to live a crucified life, we will have the peace of Jesus no matter how difficult life becomes.

God is just. He gives us resources to live the crucified, resurrected life. John Fischer explains, "The idea of dying to self and taking up your cross is one of the hardest concepts of the Christian faith to understand. It's hard not because it's complicated; it's hard because it is so difficult to accept. No one likes to die."[30]

But the other side of death to self and death to the world is resurrection life.

"Therefore, since we are surrounded by such a great cloud of witnesses, let us throw off everything that hinders and the sin that so easily entangles, and let us run with perseverance the race marked out for us. Let us fix our eyes on Jesus, the author and perfecter of our faith, who for the joy set before him endured the cross, scorning its shame, and sat down at the right hand of the throne of God" (Hebrews 12:1-2).

Jesus endured the cross for the joy set before him. When you make these daily choices to deny yourself, joy is set before you. It's a different world from clinging to yourself, placing demands on others or complaining that life is unfair.

You may ask, "How does this work?" The Holy Spirit is not only our comforter and counselor, but he will become our executioner if we allow him that function. It is the Holy Spirit who is able to "put to death the misdeeds of the body."

> "For if you live according to the sinful nature[flesh], you will die; but if by the Spirit you put to death the misdeeds of the body, you will live" (Romans 8:13).

Often I have struggled with bad habits and moral challenges. I would make resolutions to change, only to see those resolutions disappear in a couple of days. But I learned I can give bad habits and moral challenges to the Holy Spirit and cooperate with him in putting them to death.

> "I pray also that the eyes of your heart may be enlightened in order that you may know the hope to which he has called you, the riches of his glorious inheritance in the saints, and his incomparably great power for us who believe. That power is like the working of his mighty strength, which he exerted in Christ when he raised him from the dead and seated him at his right hand in the heavenly realms" (Ephesians 1:17-20).

The power that raised Jesus from the dead and seated him at the right hand of God is the same power that works in us through the Holy Spirit! The devil will come to you and say, "The way you are is the way you are always going to be. You might as well give up." But the Holy Spirit comes in power and says the future does not have to be like the past. The grace of God says it is never too late.

THE RESURRECTION

Though the cross of Christ was absolutely central and basic to the Early Church, what really fired up the faith of early believers was the resurrection. "The resurrection transformed the band of shattered disciples into people who were convinced that Jesus was alive and that they had a message that would transform the world."[31]

They became fearless witnesses, as we see in the book of Acts:

"...God raised him from the dead... because it was impossible for death to keep its hold on him" (Acts 2:24).

"...God has made this Jesus, whom you crucified, both Lord and Christ" (Acts 2:36).

"...You killed the author of life, but God raised him from the dead. We are witnesses of this" (Acts 3:15).

"...Jesus Christ of Nazareth, whom you crucified but whom God raised from the dead... With great power the apostles continued to testify to the resurrection of the Lord Jesus..." (Acts 4:10-12, 33).

"The God of our fathers raised Jesus from the dead – whom you had killed by hanging him on a tree... We are witnesses of these things, and so is the Holy Spirit..." (Acts 5:30-32).

"We are witnesses of everything he did... They killed him by hanging him on a tree, but God raised him from the dead on the third day..." (Acts 10:39-40).

"...the one whom God raised from the dead did not see decay" (Acts 13:37).

"He has given proof of this to all men by raising him from the dead" (Acts 17:31).

"They had some points of dispute with him about their own religion and about a dead man named Jesus who Paul claimed was alive" (Acts 25:18-19).

The most thrilling passage concerning this truth of the resurrected and exalted Christ is I Corinthians 15, the great resurrection chapter. Paul painted the dark picture of what it would be like for us if Christ had not been raised:

Our preaching and faith would be useless.

We would be false witnesses because we have testified of Christ being raised.

We would still be in our sins.

Then Paul declared that Christ has indeed been raised! Along with the central message of the cross, there is the great celebration of the resurrection and exaltation of Christ.

"Paul's theology is fundamentally an account of God's work of transforming his people into the image of Christ. Within the story, everything points to the death and resurrection of Jesus as the pivot-point of the ages; the old cosmos has met its end, and God's eschatological righteousness/justice has broken in upon the present, making everything new."[32]

"Christ's resurrection is the Father's verdict by the power of the Holy Spirit confirming the efficacy of the work of the cross as a judgment that brings a forgiving grace that we do not deserve and cannot earn."[33]

THE COMING OF THE HOLY SPIRIT

To Luke, the coming of the Holy Spirit in power was the turning point for the believers. They were never the same. From that point on, the early believers considered themselves to be a "Holy Spirit community."

The presence and power of the Holy Spirit is a recurring emphasis in the book of Acts:

"…Then Peter, filled with the Holy Spirit, said to them… know this, you and all the people of Israel: It is by the name of Jesus Christ of Nazareth, whom you crucified but whom God raised from the dead… " (Acts 4:5-10, esp. vs. 8).

"After they prayed, the place where they were meeting was shaken. And they were all filled with the Holy Spirit and spoke the word of God boldly" (Acts 4:31).

"Then Peter said, 'Ananias, how is it that Satan has so filled your heart that you lied to the Holy Spirit and have kept for yourself some of the money you received for the land?'" (Acts 5:3).

"Brothers, choose seven men from among you who are known to be full of the Spirit and wisdom…" (Acts 6:3, 5).

"...But Stephen, full of the Holy Spirit, looked up to heaven and saw the glory of God, and Jesus standing at the right hand of God..." (Acts 7:54-60).

"...When they arrived, they prayed for them, that they might receive the Holy Spirit, because the Holy Spirit had not yet come upon any of them; they had simply been baptized into the name of the Lord Jesus. Then Peter and John placed their hands on them, and they received the Holy Spirit..." (Acts 8:14-17).

"The Spirit told Philip, 'Go to that chariot and stay near it'" (Acts 8:29).

"While Peter was still thinking about the vision, the Spirit said to him, 'Simon, three men are looking for you'" (Acts 10:19).

"While Peter was still speaking these words, the Holy Spirit came on all who heard the message. The circumcised believers who had come with Peter were astonished that the gift of the Holy Spirit had been poured out even on the Gentiles. For they heard them speaking in tongues and praising God" (Acts 10:44-46).

"While they were worshiping the Lord and fasting, the Holy Spirit said, 'Set apart for me Barnabas and Saul for the work to which I have called them'" (Acts 13:2-3).

"God, who knows the heart, showed that he accepted them by giving the Holy Spirit to them, just as he did to us... It seemed good to the Holy Spirit and to us not to burden you with anything beyond the following requirements..." (Acts 15:8, 28-29).

"Paul and his companions traveled throughout the region... having been kept by the Holy Spirit from preaching the word in the province of Asia" (Acts 16:6).

The early Christians knew they were a Holy Spirit community and that he was presently ministering in their lives. We must have that same conviction.

The Holy Spirit is fully God. An unscriptural terminology developing in Christianity refers to the "first, second and third persons of the Trinity." This terminology, which did not arise from the Bible, gives the impression that the Holy Spirit is somehow in third place. Each person of the Trinity is fully God. When we talk about the Holy Spirit being present, we are not like the Gnostic, who spoke of some distant emanation of spirit. We are talking about GOD, a vital truth to remember.

The incarnation, the cross of Christ and its effects on our behalf, the resurrection and the outpouring of the Holy Spirit together form the basis of the New Testament church.

CHAPTER 3

SCOPE, METAPHORS AND PATTERN

SCOPE

The New Testament refers both to the **local church** and the **universal church**.

Jesus mentioned the **local church** in the matter of church discipline.

> "If he refuses to listen to them, tell it to the church; and
> if he refuses to listen even to the church..."
> (Matthew 18:17).

Paul referred to the **local church** mostly in mentioning those of a specific location.

> "To the church of God in Corinth..." (I Corinthians 1:2
> and II Corinthians 1:1)

> "To the church of the Thessalonians..."
> (I Thessalonians 1:1)

> "To the churches in Galatia..." (Galatians 1:2).

On other occasions Paul just addressed the **local church** as "saints."

Some insist that the **local church** is the only church, but Jesus spoke of the **universal church**.

> "...on this rock I will build my church..."
> (Matthew 16:18).

Paul's references to the **universal church** include

"And God placed all things under his feet and appointed him to be head over everything for the church, which is his body..." (Ephesians 1:22-23).

"And he is the head of the body, the church..." (Colossians 1:18).

The Kingdom

Jesus spoke often about the kingdom – the kingdom that has come, is coming and will come.

The church is not the same as the **kingdom**, but only a partial manifestation of the kingdom. In a church where I served as pastor, we practiced church discipline according to God's Word. One lady objected to this practice, saying, "But the Bible says in Matthew 13:24-30 to 'let the wheat and the weeds grow together until harvest.'"

The passage she referred to involves the kingdom, not the church.

The **kingdom of God** is the absolute rule and reign of God whether it is acknowledged or not. The **church** is a separate people who have chosen to submit to God's rule.

The kingdom **precedes** the church as a **universal and eternal** reality, whereas the church is a **place-in-time** reality.

The kingdom **supersedes** the church because it **both precedes** and **will follow** it.

The kingdom is the **in-break** of the authority and rule of God upon the hearts of people made in his image.

The kingdom **is arriving**, and in our response to the kingdom witness, we become the body of Christ.

God is sovereign over all. Even though the devil is called the prince of this world, he is not the sovereign of the world.[34]

METAPHORS

Among the metaphors the Bible uses for the church are

The Body	The Bride of Christ
The Temple	The Family of God

The Body

One of the most graphic metaphors describes the church as the **body** (I Corinthians 12:12-31).

"The body is a unit, though it is made up of many parts; and though all its parts are many, they form one body..." (verse 12).

"Now you are the body of Christ, and each one of you is a part of it" (verse 27).

Once when I was in a hotel coffee shop in Atlanta I saw a man who had no forearms or hands. He walked up to the cashier and paid for a newspaper by using his toes to take coins from his shoe and place them on the counter.

Sometimes the church operates that way. Like this man, we adjust and adapt in doing God's work. But how much better and easier if the man had arms and hands. In the same way, God wants every distinctive, unique part in the body to function, which is the case in a healthy church.

Paul goes into this metaphor of the church as the body in greater length in the book of Ephesians, especially 1:22-23; 3:6; 4:4, 12, 16; 5:23, 30. At the end of Ephesians 5, Paul stated pointedly, "...I am talking about Christ and the church" (verse 32).

Christ is the head of the body (the Church). In ancient physiology, the head was understood to provide all that was necessary for the life and health of the body, reflecting the relationship of Christ and his church.

As Head, Jesus is the church's Savior.

"Christ is the head of the church, his body, of which he is the Savior" (Ephesians 5:23).

As Head, Jesus is the church's Redeemer.

"...just as Christ loved the church and gave himself up for her" (Ephesians 5:25).

As Head, Jesus is the church's Cleanser and Purifier.

"...to make her holy, cleansing her by the washing with water through the word, and to present her to himself as a radiant church, without stain or wrinkle or any other blemish, but holy and blameless" (Ephesians 5:26-27).

As Head, Jesus is the church's Sovereign.
"...far above all rule and authority, power and dominion, and every title that can be given... and God placed all things under his feet and appointed him to be head over everything for the church, which is his body..."
(Ephesians 1:21-23).

As Head, Jesus is the church's Lord.
"Now as the church submits to Christ, so also wives should submit to their husbands in everything"
(Ephesians 5:24).

As Head, Jesus is the church's Sustainer.
"...husbands ought to love their wives as their own bodies... No one ever hated his own body, but he feeds and cares for it, just as Christ does the church – for we are members of his body" (Ephesians 5:28-30).

The Temple

Paul used another metaphor to describe the church as a **building (temple)**: "...you are God's field, God's building..." (I Corinthians 3:9-11).

"Don't you know that you yourselves are God's temple and that God's Spirit lives in you?" (I Corinthians 3:16).

Just as God dwelt in the Holy of Holies, God the Holy Spirit dwells not only in the church but also in individual Christians.

"Do you not know that your body is a temple of the Holy Spirit, who is in you, whom you have received from God?" (I Corinthians 6:19).

In these passages from I Corinthians we see the individual and the corporate body of Christ as the temple/building of God.

Jesus is the **cornerstone** of the building.

58

"Consequently, you are no longer foreigners and aliens, but fellow citizens with God's people and members of God's household, built on the foundation of the apostles and prophets, with Christ Jesus himself as the chief cornerstone. In him the whole building is joined together and rises to become a holy temple in the Lord. And in him you too are being built together to become a dwelling in which God lives by his Spirit" (Ephesians 2:19-22).

The cornerstone which the apostles laid in their proclamation of Jesus is the foundation of the building. Some translations say *keystone*, the stone right in the middle of the arch that holds all the stones together or a stone at the corner of a building uniting two intersecting walls. In our day a cornerstone is laid as a memorial of something, often hollowed out to contain historical documents. But in New Testament times the cornerstone was the first stone laid, followed by all the others.

These metaphors of a body and a building reflect unity and relationship. "There is no doubt that through these metaphors, especially those of the body and the building, the responsibility of each member towards other members of the community is emphasized. One part of the body cannot exist without the other parts of the body, any more than individual parts of a building can be removed without weakening the whole. This sense of social responsibility within the community is particularly strong in the New Testament teaching on love. The Christian church was intended to be a loving fellowship."[35]

The Bride of Christ

"I am jealous for you with a godly jealousy. I promised you to one husband, to Christ, so that I might present you as a pure virgin to him. But I am afraid that just as Eve was deceived by the serpent's cunning, your minds may somehow be led astray from your sincere and pure devotion to Christ" (2 Corinthians 11:2-3).

Paul used this metaphor from the Old Testament that speaks of the people of God becoming prostitutes in the spiritual sense.

Paul warned the Corinthians not to prostitute themselves by giving themselves to "...a Jesus other than the Jesus we preached... a different gospel" (II Corinthians 11:4).

> "Do you not know that your bodies are members of Christ himself? Shall I then take the members of Christ and unite them with a prostitute? Never!" (I Corinthians 6:15).

The emphasis is that the church must remain pure and loyal to its one husband, Christ. On the positive side, the bride imagery speaks of intimacy and a strong bond of love between Christ and the church.

The metaphor of the church as the bride of Christ has a very practical application to our ministry. John the Baptist said:

> "You yourselves can testify that I said, 'I am not the Christ but am sent ahead of him.' The bride belongs to the bridegroom. The friend who attends the bridegroom waits and listens for him, and is full of joy when he hears the bridegroom's voice. That joy is mine, and it is now complete. He must become greater; I must become less" (John 3:28-30).

Today he would say, "The bride (church) belongs to the bridegroom (Christ), not to me. I am simply the groomsman (best man)." John saw himself as a facilitator for the bride and the bridegroom.

In my oldest son's wedding I saw a strong illustration of keeping the bridegroom, Christ, central. My son's "best man" stayed completely focused on making sure everything went well for the joining of the groom and his bride.

As pastor, I used to see the church as "my" church, which resulted in carrying a tremendous burden. When I realized that the church belongs to Christ, I simply began to do my part in bringing the bride and the bridegroom together.

In any ministry this mentality is crucial – the people belong to the bridegroom (Christ) and not to you. When your motive is service to the bride and bridegroom, you become a better servant.

But when you think the "bride" is yours, you are tempted to be possessive and controlling. By remembering that the bride belongs to the bridegroom, you can release her. Keeping this principle in mind allows you to rest in the Lord and find freedom in your ministry.

The Family of God

The church is also the **family of God**.

"How great is the love the Father has lavished on us, that we should be called children of God! And that is what we are!" (I John 3:1).

"Because you are sons, God sent the Spirit of his Son into our hearts, the Spirit who calls out, '*Abba*, Father.' So you are no longer a slave, but a son; and since you are a son, God has made you also an heir" (Galatians 4:6-7).

"For you did not receive a spirit that makes you a slave again to fear, but you received the Spirit of sonship. And by him we cry, '*Abba*, Father.' The Spirit himself testifies with our spirit that we are God's children. Now if we are children, then we are heirs – heirs of God and co-heirs with Christ, if indeed we share in his sufferings in order that we may also share in his glory" (Romans 8:15-17).

During several bouts with clinical depression, God brought a glorious and sustaining truth to me. As I studied this whole concept of family, I became convinced that

"God is my good, loving heavenly Father.
I am his dearly loved, accepted child.
I am a part of his eternal redemptive purpose.
My Savior, Jesus, is my brother.
Every Christian is my brother or sister, too.
Heaven is my family home.
Every day I am one day nearer home."

At times when I struggled with my inadequacies, insecurities and feelings of worthlessness, I repeated this affirmation morning and evening. This practice strengthened my hold on an eternal truth which is for every believer.

Finally, because we are children and heirs of God and co-heirs with Christ, we can claim the promise of Psalm 2:6c-8:

> "'You are my Son; today I have become your Father. Ask of me, and I will make the nations your inheritance, the ends of the earth your possession."

PATTERN

> "Every day they continued to meet together in the temple courts. They broke bread in their homes and ate together with glad and sincere hearts" (Acts 2:46).

The New Testament church had both house meetings and larger congregational meetings. In the temple they probably gathered routinely in Solomon's colonnade, which ran along the east side of the outer court (Acts 3:11; 5:12). The believers met in homes and at the temple or synagogue because church buildings were not erected until the time of Constantine (b. 306 - d. 337).

The Apostle Paul frequently refers to the practice of house meetings in his letters:

> "Greet Priscilla and Aquila, my fellow workers in Christ Jesus... Greet also the church that meets at their house..." (Romans 16:3-5).

> "Give my greetings to... Nympha and the church in her house" (Colossians 4:15).

> "...to the church that meets in your home..."
> (Philemon 2).

"When a person is drawn into a little circle, devoted to prayer and to deep sharing of spiritual resources, he is well aware that he is welcomed for his own sake, since the small group has no budget, no officers concerned with the success of their administration, and nothing to promote."[36]

Even in today's church the large group and small group gatherings are practiced, but the small group offers special benefits, for instance:

1. Flexibility, mobility and inclusion
2. Natural growth through multiplication and effective means of evangelism
3. Minimum need for professional leadership and financial resources
4. A setting that encourages intimacy and vulnerability, which aid spiritual growth

In a small group or a new cell church, responsibilities can be shared, even with new Christians leading in various components of worship.

One of the greatest assets of the small group is that it requires a minimum of professional leadership and financial resources.

I had the privilege to be in a two-week cell church conference under the leadership of Dr. George Patterson, who divided the class into small groups, with each group functioning as an "underground" cell church.

A Model of a Typical Small Group or "Cell" Meeting

In each meeting one person would lead in worship, possibly reading from the Psalms in a soft voice or leading songs in a low volume. Another would quietly guide the conversational prayer time, largely consisting of praise and thanksgiving. Someone else would read the Scripture, giving a teaching if impressed by the Spirit to do so. Another person would serve the Lord's Supper.

Someone introduced the time of sharing, which offered opportunity for wide participation, from presenting personal concerns to giving testimonies. Times of confession, forgiveness and assurance often followed, then intercessory prayer.

Finally, the tithes and offerings were received. The group prayerfully sought the Spirit's leadership about the distribution of the funds collected. Responsibilities were assigned for the next meeting, always with tasks rotated among the members.

This excellent model brings each person into meaningful participation within the small group.

"The small group was the basic unit of the church's life during its first two centuries... Christians met almost exclusively in private homes... In fact, the use of small groups of one kind or another seems to be a common element in all significant movements of the Holy Spirit throughout church history. Early Pietism... the Wesleyan Revival in England... the Holiness Revival that swept America in the late 1800s... the modern Pentecostal movement."[37]

We should earnestly pray and do everything possible to see families come to personal faith in Christ. Traditionally, the emphasis has been on winning individuals to Christ, a method which has been labeled "extraction evangelism." Because the practice tends to take the individual out of his/her family and cultural context, it often exacts a great price in rejection, ostracism and other social problems. We must certainly continue to witness to individuals but also purpose to see members of their families become Christians, thus providing a built-in support group. Keeping families intact must be prominent in the thinking of church planters.

As we have seen, local church meetings were initiated in the context of the family. Every effort should be made, through teaching and example, to maintain healthy families. "If your Christianity does not work at home, don't try to export it."

I recommend that no effort be made to make the transition from an established, traditionally organized church to the cell church format. However, it is possible for vital small groups to function within the traditional structure. It requires commitment, but it can be done.

To emphasize the advantages of the cell church for church planters is by no means intended to denigrate the effectiveness of many traditionally organized churches.

PART TWO

New Testament Church Practices

Chapter One: Worship and Teaching

Chapter Two: Fellowship (Koinonia)

Chapter Three: Prayer and Fasting

Chapter Four: Water Baptism and The Lord's Supper

Chapter Five: Church Discipline

Chapter Six: Spiritual Gifts

CHAPTER 1

WORSHIP AND TEACHING

WORSHIP

Worship held a central place in the life of the Early Church. Acts 2:47 states that believers were "praising God and enjoying the favor of all the people."

Worship through Song

"Let the word of Christ dwell in you richly as you teach and admonish one another with all wisdom, and as you sing psalms, hymns and spiritual songs with gratitude in your hearts to God" (Colossians 3:16).

The **psalms** were the same biblical psalms we have in our Bible today. Probably the **hymns** were similar to our hymns and praise choruses, and the **spiritual songs** were singing in the Spirit, spontaneously using "new" words and tunes prompted by the Holy Spirit.

Some Scripture passages may have been lyrics sung in the Early Church. Some examples are Philippians 2:6-11; Colossians 1:15-20; I Timothy 3:16; and Ephesians 5:14. In fact, the first fourteen verses of Ephesians chapter one are based on a hymn sung in the Early Church. The chorus is repeated in verses 6, 12 and 14. These hymns were useful in teaching and reinforcing great truth.

Sacrifice of Praise, Sacrifice of Service

"Through Jesus, therefore, let us continually offer to God a sacrifice of praise – the fruit of lips that confess his name. And do not forget to do good and to share with others, for with such sacrifices God is pleased" (Hebrews 13:15-16).

In this passage the **sacrifice of praise** and the **sacrifice of service** go together as they always should. One without the other is deficient.

True praise is the motivation for unselfish service, and unselfish service gives credibility to praise. Biblical worship fuels a desire to serve, not just to worship. But to serve effectively, one must truly worship.

I like what Jill Briscoe says: "If you are having an experience of worship which leads only to a desire for more and more worship, you are not experiencing biblical worship. True worship leads to service, and we must truly worship if we are to truly serve."[38]

Jesus Enables Us

The sacrifice Jesus made for us enables our sacrifice of praise and service. "Through Jesus, therefore..." (verse 15). We must not miss this truth. Jesus gives us access to praise and empowerment for service. We enter the most holy place by the blood of Jesus.

> "Therefore, brothers, since we have confidence to enter the Most Holy Place by the blood of Jesus, by a new and living way opened for us through the curtain, that is, his body..." (Hebrews 10:19-20).

We must keep the cross in the center because it is central to everything.

> "For there is one God and one mediator between God and men, the man Christ Jesus" (I Timothy 2:5).

Authentic biblical praise is the fruit of "confessing God's name." *To confess his name* means to speak in accordance with it because God's name represents all that he is. We will never continually offer a sacrifice of praise until we live continually in the reality of who God is.

"...Let us continually offer to God a sacrifice of praise, the fruit of lips that confess his name" (Hebrews 13:15).

The Reality of Who God Is

The character of God could be the subject of several volumes. However, in this chapter I will focus on his qualities of

> Truth
> Love
> Holiness
> Righteousness and Justice
> Self-Existence and Unchanging Nature

First, God is **truth**.

"Jesus answered, 'I am the way and the truth and the life'" (John 14:6).

"Now this is eternal life: that they may know you, the only true God, and Jesus Christ, whom you have sent" (John 17:3).

"We know also that the Son of God has come and has given us understanding, so that we may know him who is true" (I John 5:20).

Jesus referred to the Holy Spirit as the "Spirit of truth" several times (John 14:17; 15:26; 16:13). Jesus also prayed to God the Father, "Sanctify them by the truth; your word is truth" (John 17:17).

God is objective truth. He is true in his inner nature, totally apart from us. There are no contradictions in God. All his character qualities conform to each other.

What does the character of God as truth mean in our relationship with him? When a person is truthful we can believe that what he says is true and that he will do what he says he will do. In other words, he is reliable and trustworthy.

The Apostle Paul and the writer of Hebrews declared that God does not lie.

"...God, who does not lie..." (Titus 1:2)

"...It is impossible for God to lie..." (Hebrews 6:18).

In a world full of deceit and fraud, it is reassuring to know that we have a God who is always truthful.

Because God is truth, he is a faithful person who keeps his promises.

> "You know with all your heart and soul that not one of all the good promises the Lord your God gave you has failed. Every promise has been fulfilled; not one has failed" (Joshua 23:14).

The psalmist repeatedly declared the faithfulness of God.

> "I will sing of the Lord's great love forever; with my mouth I will make your faithfulness known through all generations. I will declare that your love stands firm forever, that you established your faithfulness in heaven itself" (Psalm 89:1-2).

> "For the Lord is good and his love endures forever, his faithfulness continues through all generations"
> (Psalm 100:5).

Second, God is **love**.

> "Whoever does not love does not know God, because God is love... And so we know and rely on the love God has for us. God is love. Whoever lives in love lives in God, and God in him" (I John 4:8, 16).

The fact that God is love necessitates the triune nature of God. Love is possible only between persons. "God has in himself the eternal and wholly adequate object of his love, independently of his relation to the world."[39] As Father, Son and Holy Spirit he is perfect mutual love, mutual self-giving.

"From the Bible we learn that within God's being there is a mysterious living love, a dynamic reciprocity of surrender and affirmation, of giving and receiving, among the Father, the Son and the Holy Spirit... What makes God God is the relationship of total and mutual self-giving by which the Father gives everything to the Son and the Son offers back all that He has to glorify the Father, the love of each being established and sealed by the Holy Spirit who proceeds from both."[40]

As God who is love, he always acts in love toward us. His character is self-giving love.

"For God so loved the world that he gave his one and only Son, that whoever believes in him shall not perish but have eternal life" (John 3:16).

"This is how God showed his love among us: He sent his one and only Son into the world that we might live through him. This is love: not that we loved God, but that he loved us and sent his Son as an atoning sacrifice for our sins" (I John 4:9-10).

"This is how we know what love is: Jesus Christ laid down his life for us. And we ought to lay down our lives for our brothers" (I John 3:16).

The third aspect of God's character is **holiness**.

"Who among the gods is like you, O Lord? Who is like you – majestic in holiness, awesome in glory, working wonders?" (Exodus 15:11).

"Holy, holy, holy is the Lord Almighty; the whole earth is full of his glory" (Isaiah 6:3).

"God is pure and eternally wills and maintains his own moral purity."[41] Truth, love and holiness are who he is in his nature apart from us.

Fourth, God is a God of **righteousness** and **justice**. The Song of Moses in Deuteronomy 32 declares,

"I will proclaim the name of the Lord. Oh, praise the greatness of our God! He is the Rock, his works are perfect, and all his ways are just. A faithful God who does no wrong, upright and just is he" (Deuteronomy 32:3-4).

"Righteousness and justice are the foundation of your throne; love and faithfulness go before you. Blessed are those who have learned to acclaim you, who walk in the light of your presence, O Lord. They rejoice in your name all day long; they exult in your righteousness" (Psalm 89:14-16).

"Righteousness and justice are simply God's holiness exercised toward mankind."[42] Just as it is impossible for God to lie, it is impossible for him to contradict his holiness and act unjustly. God will never treat you unjustly. The big lie of Satan is that God is unjust. He used it with Eve in the Garden of Eden and he continues to use this same lie with all of mankind to this very day.

God acts justly when he judges sin. A holy and just God brought a flood on the world of the ungodly (Genesis 6). Upon the Second Coming of Christ, a just God

"...will punish those who do not know God and do not obey the gospel of our Lord Jesus. They will be punished with everlasting destruction and shut out from the presence of the Lord and from the majesty of his power on the day he comes to be glorified in his holy people and to be marveled at among all those who have believed. This includes you, because you believed our testimony to you" (II Thessalonians 1:8-10).

"In righteousness God reveals his love of holiness; in justice he reveals his hatred of sin."[43]

In the cross of Calvary God combined his love and holiness "...so as to be just and the one who justifies the man who has faith in Jesus" (Romans 3:26).

Fifth, God is **self-existent** and **unchanging** in his nature.

In Exodus 3, Moses asks God what His name is. God's response: "I AM WHO I AM. This is what you are to say to the Israelites: 'I AM has sent me to you.'"

Alexander McClaren wrote: "God is underived, absolute, unlimited and unalterable forever."

He is the self-existent God. God is who He is and who He has been and who He always will be.

We find no shadow of turning in God: "...the Father of the heavenly lights, who does not change like shifting shadows" (James 1:17).

God is not moody. We can be in all kinds of moods, but God is always the same. He is the I AM. You can count on his unchanging nature.

We do not evaluate God by our circumstances. We evaluate our circumstances by the character of God. The psalmist knew this when he announced, "God is good and what he does is good" (Psalm 119:68).

"Until we can come face to face with the deepest, darkest fact of life without damaging our view of God's character, we do not yet know him."[44] For more on the character of God, see Appendix 1.

What Does Knowing God's Character Produce?

True understanding of God's character will always produce enthusiastic worship from a glad and grateful heart, worship that results in service. Worship was the habitual practice of the Early Church.

Those who don't know God may think he is on an ego trip, that he simply wants everyone to focus on Him and to praise Him. But for anyone who *does* get an understanding of God's character and focuses on him, life is changed, revitalized, energized. Then God empowers our service.

"And do not forget to do good and to share with others, for with such sacrifices God is pleased" (Hebrews 13:16).

An expanded translation of this verse says not to neglect kindness, goodness and generosity. We are to do good consciously and intentionally – but not to earn God's favor. His favor is already ours because of the Cross. When our motive for doing good is to win God's favor, we don't get very far in service.

73

We make the sacrifice of service at home, at school, at work, in the streets – wherever we find ourselves. The scriptural principle is that we are to take the initiative in serving others. The active dimension of the sacrifice of service is to be alert for people who need help.

In my experience with Youth With A Mission (YWAM) I have seen this principle beautifully demonstrated. For instance, years ago when a YWAM team sought to serve in an overcrowded Vietnamese refugee camp in Hong Kong, they learned that an overused sewage system had drained several feet of sewage into the basement of one of the buildings at the camp. The team members found rubber boots, buckets and shovels and cleaned the basement.

Because the refugees saw that service and benefited from it, many accepted Jesus as Savior. In addition, government officials were so impressed that they offered a former government hospital building to be used as a YWAM base for only $1US per year.

Whole nations have opened up because Christians have served in meeting practical needs. Joe Aldridge, who for many years was president of Multnomah College of the Bible, put it this way: "People need to hear the music before they hear the words." They need to see some loving action before they can hear our verbal witness.

Sharing As Giving

In Hebrews 13:16 the verb "to share" has the same root as *koinonia*, the Greek word for "fellowship." Sharing is an expansion of doing good.

When "sharing" is used in the Bible, it can have more than one meaning. For instance, it means Holy Spirit-produced, intimate, rich, personal fellowship and communion with others. Sharing also refers to the giving and generosity that arise from that fellowship, which is its use in Hebrews 13:16. If we stop at the first meaning, we develop what Peter Wagner calls *koinonitis* – inflammatory *koinonia,* churches getting so caught up in themselves and their own relationships that strangers are left out. Churches can die from *koinonitis* and never even realize what is happening.

In II Corinthians 8:1-5 Paul expanded on sharing when he wrote about the generosity of the Macedonian churches. In verse four he said, "...they urgently pleaded with us for the privilege of sharing in this service to the saints." This beautiful example demonstrates what sharing means. The Macedonian believers shared "Out of the most severe trial... and their extreme poverty..." (verse 2). In verse 5 "...they gave themselves first to the Lord..." and then to the apostles. After giving themselves to the Lord, the rest followed.

Genuine worship includes the sacrifice of praise and the sacrifice of service, doing good and sharing with others.

TEACHING

"They devoted themselves to the apostles' teaching..." (Acts 2:42).

A body of truth must be preserved and proclaimed. For the Early Church, faith was not just the act of believing in Jesus. It was also a body of truth.

"...faith, as you were taught..." (Colossians 2:6-7).

"...the word of truth, the gospel that has come to you..." (Colossians 1:5).

"...the form of teaching to which you were entrusted..." (Romans 6:17).

Paul warned against "turning to another gospel – which is really no gospel at all" (Galatians 1:6-7) and admonished the young preacher to "continue in what you have learned and have become convinced of" (II Timothy 3:12-17).

As was noted in "Orientation," Part One, Chapter One, secular epistemology holds that there are three ways of knowing: reason, intuition and experience. As Christians we have a fourth: revelation. The body of truth God has called us to teach is his Word, the Bible.

We should use biblical terminology to teach the Word. If we use other terminology, it can be questioned. I have preached and taught in churches of various denominations – Pentecostal, Methodist, Presbyterian, Nazarene, Assemblies of God, Charismatic, Baptist, and others. When the Word of God is taught using biblical terminology and without the injection of personal opinions, that Word will produce fruit anywhere.

A popular saying is, "The Bible says it, I believe it, and that settles it." More accurately, it should be, "The Bible says it and that settles it, whether I believe it or not."

Once I spoke to the annual retreat of the Youth With A Mission (YWAM) staff in Thailand. I felt unworthy because to me they were like Mother Teresa in ministering to the poor and destitute. When I stood before them the first time, I said, "I wouldn't have the audacity to speak to you if I didn't believe in the power of God's Word and what the Holy Spirit can do with it."

With that conviction, we can preach and teach anywhere and leave the fruit up to him. We can confidently proclaim this Word, the Bible, as the body of truth.

I have been asked, "How do you bear witness in a culture where the Word of God is not really known?" My response is that you need to learn everything possible about transcultural ministry but also be firmly committed to the truth of God's Word.

> "I am not ashamed of the gospel, because it is the power of God for the salvation of everyone who believes: first for the Jew, then for the Gentile" (Romans 1:16).

CHAPTER 2

FELLOWSHIP *(KOINONIA)*

"They devoted themselves to... the fellowship" (Acts 2:42). Notice the definite article, *the* fellowship. Fellowship, one of the key themes of the New Testament, is that powerful Greek word *koinonia*, which as we have seen can also be translated *communion, community, participation, partnership* or *sharing*.

In his commentary on the book of Acts, Frank Stagg says, "It is impossible to exaggerate the importance of *koinonia*, community or fellowship. There is no more vital concept in the New Testament than that of the oneness of those who are in Christ."[45]

Koinonia has two basic dimensions: with God and with man. The two cannot be divorced. Authentic, biblical fellowship begins with fellowship with the triune God: Father, Son and Holy Spirit. The book of First John, noted for its emphasis on love, clearly focuses on *koinonia*.

"We proclaim to you what we have seen and heard, so that you also may have fellowship with us. And our fellowship is with the Father and with his Son, Jesus Christ" (I John 1:3).

Vertical *Koinonia*

Christian fellowship is anchored in fellowship with God. The Apostle Paul's benediction at the end of his second letter to the Corinthians reflects this truth.

"May the grace of the Lord Jesus Christ, and the love of God, and the fellowship of the Holy Spirit be with you all" (II Corinthians 13:14).

This fellowship is not just sharing *with* God; it is sharing *in* God. "What is at stake in the doctrine of the incarnation is the affirmation that the self-giving love of God manifested in Jesus is neither different from God the Father's creative and forgiving love nor unrelated to the communion of God's own life... Christ becomes human to draw us into the life of God's communion as Father, Son and Holy Spirit."[46]

The Apostle Paul used the phrase "in Christ" 153 times. The Apostle Peter declared that through God's divine power, glory, goodness and precious promises we may be sharers (*koinonoi*) in the divine nature (II Peter 1:3-4). Oh, the wonder of it all!

Horizontal *Koinonia*

Koinonia with God brings the inevitable corollary of *koinonia* with fellow Christians. If we pretend to have fellowship with God and have intentional broken relationships with our fellow believers, it is not *koinonia*.

The reverse is also true. If we have a grudge against God, we can't have meaningful relationships with our Christian brothers and sisters (I John 4:20). Both the vertical dimension and the horizontal dimension are included in *koinonia*, a dual fellowship seen in The Lord's Supper.

> "Is not the cup of thanksgiving for which we give thanks a participation in the blood of Christ? And is not the bread that we break a participation in the body of Christ? Because there is one loaf, we, who are many, are one body, for we all partake of the one loaf"
> (I Corinthians 10:16-17).

Koinonia binds us not only to God but also to each other, a truth that can relieve much distress in the body of Christ. Our *koinonia* in the very life of God gives rise to *koinonia* in our common life with believers. Our union with each other is based on our union with Christ.

Early Christians were not merely a society of cooperating people, but a community in the deepest sense. A society is based on function, in that a group of people who may not even know each other band together to achieve common goals.

On the other hand, a community shares a personal unity, a common life, a sense of brotherhood. Though the common life can be described by its common objectives, the community itself is not limited to these objectives.

The fellowship of the Early Church resulted not merely from cooperation.

"...Almost daily cooperation is eulogized as an ideal. In truth, cooperation in itself is not good, and it's not bad – it's a colorless neutral. Gangsters band themselves together because of a common goal, possibly to rob a bank, and they achieve cooperation in their crime. These Christians at Jerusalem were living a common life; they were not merely cooperating."[47]

Certainly, in some churches, people are united because of common goals and are identified primarily by their functions: Pastor, Sunday School teacher, Worship Minister, for examples. Such a group resembles a society more than a living organism. In such a case, people can bump into each other much like marbles rolling around in a bucket. Goals are vital, but a church needs *koinonia*.

The church that impacts the world is a *koinonia* church. The small group provides the best opportunity for experiencing *koinonia*.

A *Koinonia* Commitment

In a church that I once served as pastor, members of a cell group made the following commitment to each other:

"I want you to know that I am committed to you. You will never knowingly suffer at my hands. I will never say or do anything, knowingly, to hurt you. I will always in every circumstance seek to help you and support you. If you are down and I can lift you up, I will do that. Anything I have that you need, I will share with you, and if need be, I will give it to you. No matter what I find out about you, no matter what happens in the future, either good or bad, my commitment to you will never change. And there is nothing you can do about it. You do not have to respond. I love you, and that is what it means."[48]

To be honest, I would be hard pressed to make that commitment, but this group formally did so.

At one point one of the members discovered that his business partner had been embezzling from him. As a result, the business failed and this man was about to lose everything he had, including his home.

Another man in the cell group called me and said, "Pastor, I feel that the Holy Spirit wants me to take out a second mortgage on my house and give my friend the money so he can keep his house."

I responded, "If the Spirit is saying to do it, God will take care of it."

It developed that God provided the money in another way, so the first man did not lose his house. Nor did the other man have to take out a second mortgage on his, though he was committed to doing so if it proved necessary.

Danger! Tongue at Work

Because *koinonia* is fragile, it can easily be ruptured by careless speech. The use of the tongue is referred to more than thirty times in Proverbs.

"Reckless words pierce like a sword, but the tongue of the wise brings healing" (12:18).

"The Lord detests lying lips, but he delights in men who are truthful" (12:22).

"He who guards his lips guards his life, but he who speaks rashly will come to ruin" (13:3).

"A gentle answer turns away wrath, but a harsh word stirs up anger" (15:1).

"Even a fool is thought wise if he keeps silent, and discerning if he holds his tongue" (17:28).

The Apostle James warned of the far-reaching destructiveness of irresponsible speech. Please stop now and read chapter three in the book of James.

No Time to Criticize

A judgmental and condemning attitude toward others also breaches fellowship. Jesus warned against judging others and clearly stated the destructive results of doing so. (Read Matthew 7:1-5.)

Oswald Chambers wrote, "God gives us discernment in the lives of others to call us to intercession, never that we may find fault with them."[49]

Criticizing others reflects two improper ways of handling guilt:

1. Cast blame on someone else to "balance the scales" because of one's own guilt. The unconscious expectation is that criticizing someone else will lift the weight of guilt from oneself, demonstrating that "I'm not so bad after all."

2. The second is assuming a victim mentality. "Whoever can claim the status of victim with greater authority wins, because that status projects an image of innocence over against which all others are somehow guilty... It is society, or my parents, or my disease, or all three, and more, that are responsible for the way I am; so I am encouraged to abdicate responsibility... "[50]

Both devices vanish in a mature disciple who assumes total and complete self-responsibility.

Holding on to Hurts

Other enemies of *koinonia* are resentment and unforgiveness. Poeman, an early Desert Father, said "You can no more hide a small hurt in your heart than you can hide a small fire in hay."

"See to it that no one misses the grace of God and that no bitter root grows up to cause trouble and defile many" (Hebrews 12:15).

Resentment not only damages fellowship but it also does immeasurable physical damage to the person who harbors it.

Dr. S. I. McMillen tells of "a Christian woman who loved the Lord and who worked full time for the Lord" who developed a life-threatening ulcer because of her "restless resentment."[51] He lists a catalogue of illnesses that can be produced by emotional stress, resentment and anger.

Resentment is like drinking poison and waiting for the other person to die. "...Spiritual passion cannot coexist with resentment."[52]

Koinonia is God's gift, never man's achievement, but it demands that we live as a forgiven and forgiving community. A primary Greek word for forgiveness, *aphiemi,* literally means "to send away" or "to loose." In New Testament times it was used in the cancellation of debts, denoting that nothing further was owed.

Christian forgiveness originates with God.

"In him (Christ) we have redemption through his blood, the forgiveness of sins in accordance with the riches of God's grace" (Ephesians 1:7).

"Forgiveness rests on the atoning work of Christ because it is an act of sheer grace."[53]

The New Testament makes clear that the forgiven sinner must forgive. Jesus tells us to pray, "Forgive us our debts, as we also have forgiven our debtors" (Matthew 6:12). "Forgiving someone who has offended us releases him from needing to repay us, give compensation, or even say he is sorry."[54]

"Bear with each other and forgive whatever grievances you may have against one another. Forgive as the Lord forgave you. And over all these virtues put on love, which binds them all together in perfect unity" (Colossians 3:13-14).

How Do We Forgive?

Though forgiveness often comes slowly and with difficulty, it is possible. But how?

1. Remember how much we've been forgiven by God. Jesus gives this example in his parable of the unmerciful servant (Matthew 18:21-35).

"The parable of the unforgiving servant tells us that those who are forgiven by God must be transformed by that forgiveness into people who embody forgiveness and repentance throughout their lives... From the Christian perspective, forgiveness is not primarily a word that is spoken, or an action that is performed, or a feeling that is felt; it is a way of life appropriate to the fact that we have been forgiven by God."[55]

"The fundamental orientation of the Christian life is that we are forgiven."[56]

"...we trivialize God's forgiveness by individualizing it so that it leaves our relations with others essentially untouched."[57]

2. Recognize that forgiveness is both a choice of the will and a process. Forgiveness is not "a one-shot deal" because the emotions must catch up with the act of the will.

Charles Cerling gives five tests to verify that forgiveness is complete:[58]

   A. Can you thank God for the lessons learned during the pain?
   B. Can you talk about your hurt without getting angry, without feeling resentful, without the slightest thought of revenge?
   C. Are you willing to accept your part of the blame for what happened?
   D. Can you revisit the scene or the people involved in your hurt without experiencing a negative reaction?
   E. Can you do good to those who hurt you?

3. We can forgive by the grace of God. I use the following definition of grace:

"Grace is the righteous, self-giving, self-sacrificing personal love of God expressed to mankind. It is initiated by God the Father, made personally available through God the Son, and supernaturally applied by God the Holy Spirit. Grace is the empowering presence of God which enables us to be who God created us to be and to do what God called us to do."

If we believe this definition of grace, we CAN forgive. It is the devil who insists that we have a right to hold onto unforgiveness. Don't let him deceive you.

Lewis Smedes observes that "To forgive is to set the prisoner free and discover that the prisoner was you."[59]

"The purpose of forgiveness is not simply to heal the guilt of the sinner but the purpose of all love: to come into communion."[60] This communion is lived out in the New Testament *"one another"* sayings found in Appendix 2.

The Positive Side

The unity of Christian fellowship is nurtured by humility, gentleness and patience, the fruit of the Spirit as God forms the love of Christ in us. In humility, Jesus lived in self-forgetfulness and self-giving (Ephesians 4:2-3, Galatians 5:22-23, Philippians 2:3-8). In our daily speech and actions we must affirm the prayer of Jesus:

> "My prayer is not for them alone. I pray also for those who will believe in me through their message, that all of them may be one, Father, just as you are in me and I am in you. May they also be in us so that the world may believe that you have sent me. I have given them the glory that you gave me, that they may be one as we are one: I in them and you in me. May they be brought to complete unity to let the world know that you sent me and have loved them even as you have loved me." (John 17:20-23).

The desire of our Lord should be more than sufficient motivation to be fully committed to "Make every effort to keep the unity of the Spirit through the bond of peace" (Ephesians 4:3).

Koinonia requires that we live transparently.

84

"For you were once darkness, but now you are light in the Lord. Live as children of light (for the fruit of the light consists in all goodness, righteousness and truth) and find out what pleases the Lord. Have nothing to do with the fruitless deeds of darkness, but rather expose them. For it is shameful even to mention what the disobedient do in secret. But everything exposed by the light becomes visible" (Ephesians 5:8-13).

Darkness in this passage is associated with secrecy. To live in the light means that you live transparently: without secrets and with nothing to hide. There is great freedom in having no secrets that you fear may be discovered.

The early Christians prayed standing up with their arms outstretched to signify three things:

1. The death of Christ on the cross
2. Identification with the cross of Christ
3. Absolute openness and transparency.

God desires us to have exactly the same life he has, living in a self-giving community of love just as he lives in his own being.

Satan wants us to have his kind of existence – just as isolated, separated, alone and without meaningful relationships as he is.

The choice is ours. The Apostle Paul said,

"I have forgiven in the sight of Christ for your sake, in order that Satan might not outwit us. For we are not unaware of his schemes" (II Corinthians 2:10-11).

We must stay alert to Satan's schemes. And I pray to God that we all may be aware of God's glorious purpose for his church: fellowship (*koinonia*), in the complete biblical meaning of the word.

Generosity and Mutual Care

Immediately after Pentecost, as needs arose, the mutual sharing of resources became a primary expression of New Testament fellowship (*koinonia*) See Acts 2:44-45 and 4:32-37. The principle seemed to be, "From everyone according to his ability to everyone according to his need."

As the flame of the Spirit began to burn a little lower, difficulties with this practice developed as told in the passage of Acts 5:1-11. Ananias and Sapphira kept a part of the money they received from selling property and then lied to Peter about it.

No one required them to give their money. The Apostle Peter clearly acknowledged the right of private ownership by saying, "Didn't it belong to you before it was sold? And after it was sold, wasn't the money at your disposal?" The early Christians never sought to equalize believers economically, as twentieth century Communism claimed to do. Instead, the Christians' mutual sharing was intended only to meet community needs.

Giving which is motivated by the Holy Spirit is evident throughout the New Testament. A notable passage in the eighth and ninth chapters of II Corinthians gives five principles.

1) **Generosity:** Paul said of the Macedonians, "...out of the most severe trial, their overflowing joy and their extreme poverty welled up in rich generosity" (8:2).

2) **Procedure:** "...they gave themselves first to the Lord..." (8:5).

3) **Motivation:** "For you know the grace of our Lord Jesus Christ, that though he was rich, yet for your sakes he became poor, so that you through his poverty might become rich" (8:9).

4) **Reciprocity**, the principle of giving and receiving: "Remember this: Whoever sows sparingly will also reap sparingly, and whoever sows generously will also reap generously. Each man should give what he has decided in his heart to give, not reluctantly or under compulsion, for God loves a cheerful giver. And God is able to make all grace abound to you, so that in all things at all times, having all that you need, you will abound in every good work" (9:6-8).

5) **Blessing and thanksgiving:** "...You will be made rich in every way so that you can be generous on every occa-

sion, and through us your generosity will result in thanksgiving to God" (9:10-15).

These verses refer to a special collection for the impoverished Christians in Jerusalem. Their need may have developed because of the famine recorded in Acts 11:28 (A.D. 44 or 46) or because of persecution. Whatever the cause, the young believers in Macedonia gave generously.

How Much is Enough?

The New Testament does not state the exact amount given on a regular basis by the early believers, but the late Dr. Stephen Olford provides some insight:

"Instructed Christians would know that under the law the Jew was bound to give one-tenth of his income to God. Then, of course, there were freewill offerings, trespass offerings, and costly journeys to the temple. It has been estimated that the aggregate of religious gifts among the Jews in olden times could not have been less than one-fifth of each man's income, and some very probably involved one-third of it...

"If the Old Testament saints, under law, could give amounts of this kind, can we, under grace, give God any less? So the New Testament leaves this matter wide open for us to act in proportion to the prospering of God. "[61]

CHAPTER 3

PRAYER AND FASTING

PRAYER

"They devoted themselves...to prayer" (Acts 2:42).

A reading of the New Testament reveals the centrality of prayer in the Early Church. From the very beginning believers prayed.

Luke wrote that soon after the ascension of Jesus **"They all joined together constantly in prayer"** (Acts 1:14). After Peter's escape from prison he went to a house **"where many people had gathered and were praying"** (Acts 12:12). Before the believers at Antioch sent out Paul and Barnabas they **"fasted and prayed"** (Acts 13:3). In prison **Paul and Silas prayed** and sang hymns to God and "at once all the prison doors flew open" (Acts 16:26).

God responds to prayer. Space does not permit listing all the Scripture references in which the Apostle Paul pledged his prayers for his readers and requested their prayers for him. In fact, more than once he included prayers in his letters (Ephesians 1:15-19; 3:14-20; Philippians 1:9-11; Colossians 1:9-14, are examples).

In devoting themselves to prayer, the believers followed Jesus' example. He prayed in the morning (Mark 1:35), in the evening (Mark 6:46-47) and sometimes all night (Luke 6:12). No matter how demanding his ministry, prayer was always a priority.

"But the news about Him continued to spread, and great crowds were gathering to hear Him and to be cured of their diseases. But Jesus Himself continued His habit of retiring to lonely spots and praying" (Luke 5:15-16, Williams).

Jesus prayed before and after ministry times. He also prayed before major decisions. For instance, he prayed all night before designating the apostles (Luke 6:12-13). As he prayed in his life, he prayed even in his death: "Father, forgive them..." (Luke 23:34). Even though he was the Son of God in the flesh, his prayer habits acknowledged his total dependence upon God the Father and his constant desire to have intimate fellowship with him.

The Model for Prayer

After observing Jesus praying, a disciple requested, "Lord, teach us to pray..." (Luke 11:1). In response Jesus gave the disciples, and us, the reasons to pray and the ideal model for comprehensive praying.[62]

The purposes of prayer as found in Matthew 6:9-13 (KJV) are:

1. To build a relationship with God as Father, *"Our Father which art in heaven."*
2. To glorify God in praise and thanksgiving, *"Hallowed be Thy name."*
3. To participate in the divine activity of intercession, *"Thy kingdom come. Thy will be done in earth, as it is in heaven."*
4. To recognize and declare our total dependence upon God daily, *"Give us this day our daily bread."*
5. To seek forgiveness and to forgive, to make relationships right, *"Forgive us our debts as we forgive our debtors."*
6. To seek divine guidance and protection, *"Lead us not into temptation, but deliver us from evil."*
7. To declare God's lordship and sovereignty over all, *"For Thine is the kingdom, and the power, and the glory, forever. Amen."*

Our Father

Our Father which art in heaven (literally, "Our Father in the heavens"): To pray "our Father" is to recognize that God is personal and not some distant impersonal force. It also implies that he is loving. When Jesus compared earthly fathers with the Father in heaven, he used the words "how much more" (Matthew 7:11).

Jesus came to reveal God as Father. "You sum up the whole of New Testament teaching in a single phrase, if you speak of it as a revelation of the Fatherhood of the holy Creator. In the same way, you sum up the whole of New Testament religion if you describe it as the knowledge of God as one's holy Father... For everything that Christ taught, everything that makes the New Testament new, and better than the Old, everything that is distinctively Christian as opposed to merely Jewish, is summed up in the knowledge of the Fatherhood of God. 'Father' is the Christian name for God."[63]

A foundational conviction for effective Christian prayer is that God is a good, loving Father who can be fully trusted and is constantly working for our good. If we cannot say with the Psalmist, "You are good, and what you do is good" (Psalm 119:68), our prayers will always be flawed. The Apostle Paul prayed,

> "I keep asking that the God of our Lord Jesus Christ, the glorious Father, may give you the Spirit of wisdom and revelation, so that you may know him better" (Ephesians 1:17).

As God answers this prayer in our lives, our prayers become an ongoing and growing love relationship with God the Father, a privileged position that comes through faith in Christ.

> "You are all sons of God through faith in Christ Jesus" (Galatians 3:26).

> "The words 'in the heavens' denote not the place of his abode so much as the authority and power at his command as the creator and ruler of all things. Thus he combines fatherly love with heavenly power, and what his love directs his power is able to perform."[64]

Honoring God's Name

Hallowed be Thy name: Real prayer begins with worship and adoration. Much of contemporary Christianity starts with self and not with God. Authentic Christian praying begins with God. "Thy name... Thy kingdom... Thy will."

"Prayer is not primarily a means of getting something done, it is a concern for the glory of God."[65]

God's name equals God's nature. In Scripture the name of God is always an expression of his character. "God's 'name' is God himself as he is in himself and has revealed himself."[66] As we begin to know God's character, the inevitable response is praise for who he is and thanksgiving for what he does.

"Let the name of the Lord be praised, both now and forevermore. From the rising of the sun to the place where it sets, the name of the Lord is to be praised" (Psalm 113:2-3).

To hallow God's name with our lips is incomplete without the constant desire to honor his name with our lives. A loose paraphrase of this request could be, "May your nature – who you are – be acknowledged, respected, honored, kept holy and revealed in my life and in the lives of others."

Serious Questions to Ponder

When we ask God to hallow his name, the question follows: "Can I write 'hallowed be thy name' over my speech, the television I watch, the movies I see, the books I read, the places I go, the friends I keep?"

"What is in my life and home that does not fit the label 'Holy unto the Lord'?"

On one occasion our family was impressed to remove from our home any object that did not clearly honor the Lord. For example, on our den wall was a beautiful handcrafted brass disk, three feet in diameter, which we brought from Latin America. A friend pointed out that it had images of a pagan sun god that we had not noticed previously. We removed the disk and destroyed it. Our sons removed some music tapes, along with a number of other items. After this "cleansing," even our guests commented about the sense of God's peace in our home.

May it never be said of us what Paul said of the Pharisees of his day, "God's name is blasphemed among the Gentiles because of you" (Romans 2:24). In Jesus' prayer to God the Father he said, "I have manifested thy name..." (John 17:6, KJV). May each of us have a passion to do the same.

God's Kingdom

Thy kingdom come: The Kingdom of God exists in several dimensions.

1. **His sovereign rule over all his creation:** Over mankind, nature, history and time God does and will do anything he chooses, with or without the cooperation of mankind. He is Lord.

2. **The present aspect of the kingdom on earth, initiated by the incarnation of Christ:** John the Baptist announced, "Repent, for the kingdom of heaven is near" (Matthew 3:2). Later Jesus made the same declaration "Repent, for the kingdom of heaven is near" (Matthew 4:17). In this statement Jesus was saying the kingdom had come in him and with him. He declared the kingdom was already present in his own person and ministry, expressed through his miraculous power in healing, deliverance and the forgiveness of sin.

When John the Baptist sent his disciples to Jesus to inquire if he were the one to usher in the Messianic reign,

> "Jesus replied, 'Go back and report to John what you hear and see: The blind receive sight, the lame walk, those who have leprosy are cured, the deaf hear, the dead are raised, and the good news is preached to the poor'" (Matthew 11:4-5).

Jesus said, "If I drive out demons by the Spirit of God, then the kingdom of God has come upon you" (Matthew 12:28). In the next verse, Matthew 12:29, Jesus announced that he had entered the house of the "strong man" (Satan) and tied him up, meaning that Jesus not only had the power to heal and deliver, but also the power to forgive sins. The teachers of the law challenged Jesus when they heard him say to the paralytic, "Son, your sins are forgiven" (Mark 2:5). He responded,

"Which is easier to say to the paralytic, 'Your sins are forgiven,' or to say, 'Get up, take your mat and walk'? But that you may know that the Son of Man has authority on earth to forgive sin... ' He said to the paralytic, 'I tell you, get up, take your mat and go home'" (Mark 2:9-11).

Kingdom power was bestowed upon the twelve disciples when Jesus commissioned them, giving them "power and authority to drive out all demons and to cure diseases, and he sent them out to preach the kingdom of God and to heal the sick" (Luke 9:1-2).

Jesus also sent out a group of seventy-two who returned and joyfully exclaimed, "Lord, even the demons submit to us in your name" (Luke 10:17).

Jesus replied, "I saw Satan fall like lightning from heaven" (Luke 10:18). In other words, "the power of Satan is broken."

The kingdom has been inaugurated but has not yet been consummated. We live between "the already" and "the not yet."

According to John 14:12, our privilege as believers is to proclaim and demonstrate this gospel of the kingdom with the full expectation that God will work mightily, to His glory.

3. **The future aspect of the Kingdom:** Jesus will return in power and glory and God's purpose will be realized,

"...to bring all things in heaven and on earth together, under one head, even Christ" (Ephesians 1:10).

"...At the name of Jesus every knee should bow, in heaven and on earth and under the earth, and every tongue confess that Jesus Christ is Lord, to the glory of God the Father" (Philippians 2:10-11).

"...The kingdom of the world has become the kingdom of our Lord and of his Christ, and he will reign for ever and ever" (Revelation 11:15).

When we pray, "Thy Kingdom come," we express a longing for the Second Coming of Christ and the consummation of the Kingdom of God.

> "Now there is in store for me the crown of righteousness, which the Lord, the righteous Judge, will award to me on that day – and not only to me, but also to all who have longed for his appearing" (II Timothy 4:8).

God's Will

Thy will be done in earth, as it is in heaven: Question 98 of the Westminster Shorter Catechism asks: "What is prayer?" The first part of the answer reads, "Prayer is an offering up of our desires unto God, for things agreeable to His will... "

"However sincere the desire, however devout the forms of the words, a petition is not prayer unless God and the doing of His will are at the center of it.

"Most of the bitterness of unanswered prayer comes from the assumption that God will juggle His universe to give us what we plead for if we plead long enough."[67]

"The object of all true praying, you see, is not to bend the will of God to mine, but to get my will in line with his. True praying is not overcoming God's reluctance but laying hold of his willingness. Real prayer does not begin by attempting to persuade God to do something contrary to his will... Prayer is not primarily a means of getting something done; it is a concern for the glory of God."[68]

Heaven is characterized by obedience.

> "Praise the Lord, you his angels, you mighty ones who
> do his bidding, who obey his word" (Psalm 103:20).

When we pray, "Thy kingdom come. Thy will be done in earth, as it is in heaven," we are praying for ourselves that King Jesus will have absolute control over us and we are expressing the desire to obey him in all areas of our lives. Further, we are asking that the rule and will of God may prevail in more and more lives across the world.

"Thy will be done" is the prayer that never fails. With faith we can pray this for all the nations "in earth."

"In the ongoing work of the kingdom of God, nothing is more important than Intercessory Prayer... Intercessory Prayer is priestly ministry... As priests, appointed and anointed by God, we have the honor of going before the Most High on behalf of others. This is not optional; it is a sacred obligation – and a precious privilege – of all who take up the yoke of Christ."[69]

Scriptural praying is an effort to conform our minds to the mind of Christ. Sometimes I do not know what I should specifically pray, but I can pray "thy will be done" with confidence because of the Holy Spirit's ministry.

> "In the same way, the Spirit helps us in our weakness. We do not know what we ought to pray for, but the Spirit himself intercedes for us with groans that words cannot express. And he knows the mind of the Spirit, because the Spirit intercedes for the saints in accordance with God's will. And we know that in all things God works for the good of those who love him, who have been called according to his purpose" (Romans 8:26-28).

We are not to place our faith in our prayers, but in the God to whom we pray, the Father of love and power who always works for our good. Faith is believing that God is who he claims to be, that his Word is true and that he will do what he says he will do.

> "For we have heard of your faith in Christ Jesus [the leaning of your entire human personality on Him in absolute trust and confidence in His power, wisdom and goodness] and of the love which you [have and show] for all the saints (God's consecrated ones)" (Colossians 1:4, AMP).

God's Provision

Give us this day our daily bread asks for God's provision.

"In the middle of the Lord's Prayer there is a distinct division. You see it in the pronouns. In the first three petitions we are taught to say 'Thy,' 'Thy name,' 'Thy kingdom,' 'Thy will.' But in the last three petitions are 'us' and 'our.' First, we think of God, then we can rightfully think of ourselves."[70]

The request is "Give *us*," not "Give *me*." Even in prayer for our daily necessities we must remember the needs of others. Nothing is too small or too great to bring to God. We depend on God for food and all our daily necessities. This request could be paraphrased to read, "Give us all that we need for today."

No Anxiety about the Future

"Give us this day" indicates living one day at a time. We are saying that God's provision for today is enough; we will not worry about the future. The person of faith lives in the "precious present," a position that does not exclude responsible planning, but does exclude worry.

> "Therefore I tell you, do not worry about your life, what you will eat or drink; or about your body, what you will wear. Is not life more important than food, and the body more important than clothes? Look at the birds of the air; they do not sow or reap or store away in barns, and yet your heavenly Father feeds them. Are you not much more valuable than they? Who of you by worrying can add a single hour to his life? And why do you worry about clothes? See how the lilies of the field grow. They do not labor or spin. Yet I tell you that not even Solomon in all his splendor was dressed like one of these. If that is how God clothes the grass of the field, which is here today and tomorrow is thrown into the fire, will he not much more clothe you, O you of little faith? So do not worry, saying, 'What shall we eat?' or 'What shall we wear?' For the pagans run after all these things, and your heavenly Father knows that you need them. But seek first his kingdom and his righteousness, and all these things will be given to you. Therefore do not worry about tomorrow, for tomorrow will worry about itself. Each day has enough trouble of its own" (Matthew 6:25-34).

Complete daily dependence upon God does not presume laziness. It is our responsibility to "gather up" what God provides. Writing of God's creatures, "both large and small," the Psalmist said,

> "These all look to you to give them their food at the proper time. When you give it to them, they gather it up; when you open your hand, they are satisfied with good things" (Psalm 104:27-28).

No regret about the Past

Many of us not only worry about the future, we also live in regret about the past. We drag yesterday and tomorrow into today, robbing ourselves of the present and reducing our effectiveness in Kingdom service. Oswald Chambers encourages us to "...let the past sleep, but let it sleep in the sweet embrace of Christ, and let us go on into the invincible future with Him."[71]

Generally, the struggle with the past has to do with past sins. "If the Lord Jesus Christ has washed you in his own blood and forgiven you all your sins, how dare you refuse to forgive yourself."[72]

When living in anticipation or in memory, we neglect the present moment. Living in the world of "if only" and "what if" creates overriding anxiety, a common plague of the modern world.

God calls us to live in the opposite spirit. "The glory of the gospel is that when the Church is absolutely different from the world, she invariable attracts it."[73]

"God wants us to move through this day with a quiet heart, an inward assurance that He is in control, a peaceful certainty that our lives are in His hands, a deep trust in His plan and purposes, and a thankful disposition toward all that He allows."[74] This comes only through humility, faith and glad obedience to God.

If we extract this petition from the rest of the model prayer, we see God only as the great "Need-Meeter in the sky," but God is infinitely more, as we see in the remainder of the prayer.

Living in Forgiveness[75]

Forgive us our debts as we forgive our debtors: This is the only portion of the model prayer that Jesus expanded.

"For if you forgive men when they sin against you, your heavenly Father will also forgive you. But if you do not forgive men their sins, your Father will not forgive your sins" (Matthew 6:14-15).

This troublesome statement seems to say that we earn God's forgiveness by forgiving others, which is inconsistent with the balance of the New Testament witness. The verse does not say, "Forgive us our debts because we forgive our debtors." It does not say "I forgive. God forgives," as if God forgives on an exchange basis. Salvation forgiveness deals with the sin nature. The comprehensive forgiveness of God relates to fellowship, which daily sins disrupt.

The late Bertha Smith, a much admired missionary to China, frequently greeted others with the question, "Are your sins confessed up to date?" She knew that our unhindered fellowship with God is essential to fully experience his presence and power. A forgiving spirit is a primary proof of God's forgiveness of us and one of the chief signs of true penitence. "The Christian who always lives at the cross in penitence is the Christian who always lives in fellowship with his Lord in power."[76]

Protection in Warfare

Lead us not into temptation, but deliver us from evil: God is not an active agent in subjecting us to temptation. James 1:13 says that God cannot tempt us to evil. Grammarians call the Greek verb *eisenegkes*, translated "lead," a permissive passive form. The idea is, "Do not allow us to be led into temptation, but deliver us from the evil one." Thus, the Williams translation reads, "And do not let us be subjected to temptation, but save us from the evil one," with "evil one" perhaps referring to the devil or perhaps to an evil man who seeks to do us harm.[77]

In this prayer we are agreeing with the prayer of Jesus, "My prayer is not that you take them out of the world but that you protect them from the evil one" (John 17:15).

As believers, we are in spiritual warfare. Satan exists and is the mortal enemy of every Christian, but as noted in the discussion on Satan in "Orientation," (Part One, Chapter One), he is a **defeated** foe. We stand against Satan on the basis of Christ's victory over him.

> "How I praise You that 'I need not strive toward a possible victory, but can live from a position of victory already won'... that although Satan is powerful, he cannot prevail against the blood of the Lamb and the Name of our Lord Jesus Christ. Thank You that Satan must retreat before that Name and before Your Word, the living and powerful sword of the Spirit... and that in the end he will be cast down into everlasting defeat and shame."[78]

Satan has limited power but he has *no authority* in the life of the believer. Spiritual authority is found in the Name of Jesus. We can confidently invoke the Name of Jesus against Satan and his demons. As someone has said, "It's a serious mistake to underestimate the power of Satan; it's a tragedy to overestimate it." When we pray "deliver us from the evil one" we're asserting that, though we are to be engaged in the battle, it is God who delivers us.

When King Jehoshaphat was commanded to go into battle, he was assured, "...the battle is not yours, but God's" (II Chronicles 20:15). We have a completely trustworthy promise from God's Word:

> "No temptation has seized you except what is common to man. And God is faithful; he will not let you be tempted beyond what you can bear. But when you are tempted, he will also provide a way out so that you can stand up under it" (I Corinthians 10:13).

Kingdom, Power and Glory

For thine is the kingdom, and the power, and the glory, forever. Amen. Though these concluding words do not appear in the earlier Greek manuscripts, they reflect the spirit of the entire Bible. Similar prayers are found in the Jewish writings. For example, "for the kingdom is thine and thou shalt reign in glory forever and ever."[79] The usual response at the reading of the Shemah, (Deuteronomy 6:4-9), instead of "amen" was: "Blessed be the name of the glory of his kingdom for ever and ever."[80]

In this conclusion we declare God's lordship and sovereignty over all. Our confidence that God will answer this model prayer is based on God's supreme authority and power. The Christians of the New Testament devoted themselves to prayer. We can do no less.

FASTING

Fasting was practiced by the New Testament church, as well as during Old Testament times:

Moses fasted for forty days and nights (Exodus 34:28).

David fasted for the life of his child (II Samuel 12:16).

"Jehoshaphat resolved to inquire of the Lord, and he proclaimed a fast for all of Judah" (II Chronicles 20:3).

Ezra wrote, "I proclaimed a fast so that we might humble ourselves before our God and ask him for a safe journey for us and our children, with all our possessions" (Ezra 8:21).

Esther requested that her people join her in fasting before she went to King Xerxes to plead the cause of the Israelites: "...fast for me. Do not eat or drink for three days, night or day" (Esther 4:16).

Daniel fasted and prayed to receive insight, understanding and revelation. "I turned to the Lord God and pleaded with him in prayer and petition, in fasting, and in sackcloth and ashes" (Daniel 9:3).

The Old Testament prophets denounced any fasting that was inconsistent with God's purposes. Jeremiah recited the sins of the people and declared "Then the Lord said to me, 'Do not pray for the well-being of this people. Although they fast, I will not listen to their cry...'" (Jeremiah 14:12). Isaiah rebuked the Israelites for fasting while at the same time forsaking the commands of God. Then he described God's chosen fast:

"Is not this the kind of fasting I have chosen: to loose the chains of injustice and untie the cords of the yoke, to set the oppressed free and break every yoke? Is it not to share your food with the hungry and to provide the poor wanderer with shelter – when you see the naked, to clothe him, and not to turn away from your own flesh and blood? Then your light will break forth like the dawn, and your healing will quickly appear; then your righteousness will go before you, and the glory of the Lord will be your rear guard. Then you will call, and the Lord will answer; you will cry for help, and he will say: Here am I" (Isaiah 58:6-9).

When the people of Nineveh fasted, God withheld judgment against them:

> "The Ninevites believed God. They declared a fast, and all of them, from the greatest to the least, put on sack-cloth... When God saw what they did and how they turned from their evil ways, he had compassion and did not bring upon them the destruction he had threatened" (Jonah 3:5, 10).

The only recorded occasion of Jesus fasting was at the time of his temptations in the desert (Matthew 4:1-11), but he assumed that the disciples would fast. He said to them, "when you fast," not "if you fast" (Matthew 6:16-18).

In Acts, leaders of the church fasted when choosing missionaries (13:2-3) and elders (14:23).

John Stott asserts, "I suspect that some of us live our Christian lives as if these verses had been torn out of our Bibles." He adds, "There can be no doubt that in Scripture fasting has to do in various ways with self-denial and self-discipline."[81]

In Titus chapter two, Paul told Titus what to teach to various age-groups. In every case, Paul's instructions included self-control, that is, the control of our bodies and appetites.

Paul also used a metaphor from the sport of boxing, "...I beat my body and make it my slave so that after I have preached to others, I myself will not be disqualified for the prize" (I Corinthians 9:27).

"This is neither masochism (finding pleasure in self-inflicted pain), nor false asceticism (like wearing a hair shirt or sleeping on a bed of spikes), nor an attempt to win merit like the Pharisee in the temple (Luke 18:12). Paul would reject all such ideas, and so must we. We have no cause to 'punish' our bodies (for they are God's creation), but must discipline them to make them obey us. And fasting (a voluntary abstinence from food) is one way of increasing our self-control."[82]

God's Chosen Fast by Arthur Wallis is a modern book on this ancient but relevant practice. Some of the reasons he suggests for fasting are

1. To minister to the Lord
2. To heighten understanding of the Scripture
3. To express humility and dependence upon God
4. To appeal for special needs
5. To loose men from bondage
6. To gain wisdom and guidance
7. To request protection and safety.[83]

"The evidence is plain that special enterprises need special prayer, and that special prayer may well involve fasting."[84]

NOTE: Campus Crusade for Christ International has suggestions on how to fast. On the internet go to *www.ccci.org*. Click on "Spiritual Growth." Under "Additional Resources" you will find helps on fasting and prayer.

CHAPTER 4

WATER BAPTISM AND THE LORD'S SUPPER

WATER BAPTISM

Three water baptisms are mentioned in the New Testament.

The Baptism of John the Baptist

The baptism of John the Baptist, may have arisen from the Jewish proselyte baptism – a rite of initiation for Gentile converts. However, the emphasis of John's baptism was different from that of Jewish proselyte baptism. The Gentile convert faced three requirements: circumcision, baptism and a sacrificial offering. After the destruction of the temple in 70 A.D., the requirement of the sacrifice was eliminated. Later, because many women came into the Jewish faith, less importance was made of circumcision. So the focal point of conversion from Gentile to Jew became baptism.

John's baptism also differed from the proselyte baptism in that he baptized those who were already Jews, but Jews whom John regarded as aliens to true Israel. This baptism was one of repentance. Because John did not consider them to be the people of the Messiah, he called them to repent and return to God.

"But when he saw many of the Pharisees and Sadducees coming to where he was baptizing, he said to them: 'You brood of vipers! Who warned you to flee from the coming wrath? Produce fruit in keeping with repentance. And do not think you can say to yourselves, 'We have Abraham as our father.' I tell you that out of these stones God can raise up children for Abraham'" (Matthew 3:7-9).

The Greek word for repentance, *metanoeo*, means a "change of mind". John had in mind the fuller meaning of the Jewish word for repentance, *nacham*, which included the meaning "to turn about." He required the Jewish people to have a change of mind about their relationship with God and to have a moral change as well.

John's goal was more than reform. He proclaimed the coming of the Lord and prepared the way for the Messiah.

"I baptize you with water for repentance. But after me will come one who is more powerful than I, whose sandals I am not fit to carry..." (Matthew 3:11).

The Baptism of Jesus

The second baptism in the New Testament is the baptism of Jesus.

"Then Jesus came from Galilee to the Jordan to be baptized by John. But John tried to deter him, saying, 'I need to be baptized by you, and do you come to me?' Jesus replied, 'Let it be so now; it is proper for us to do this to fulfill all righteousness.' Then John consented. As soon as Jesus was baptized, he went up out of the water. At that moment heaven was opened, and he saw the Spirit of God descending like a dove and lighting on him. And a voice from heaven said, 'This is my Son, whom I love; with him I am well pleased'" (Matthew 3:13-17).

Jesus was not baptized as an act of repentance from sin, but as a public declaration of his submission to the will of the Father. His use of the phrase "to fulfill all righteousness" declared the beginning of all he would do in the full work of redemption.

God the Father pronounced his approval of the mission of Jesus, which was tied to Old Testament prophecy about the coming of the Messiah. The Father's voice said, "...You are my son, whom I love; with whom I am well pleased" (Mark 1:11), combining two Old Testament passages:

> "...You are my Son; today I have become your Father" (Psalm 2:7).

> "Here is my servant, whom I uphold, my chosen one in whom I delight..." (Isaiah 42:1).

Jesus' later statement about the ministry of the Holy Spirit reflected his own ministry:

> "When he comes, he will convict the world of guilt in regard to sin and righteousness and judgment; in regard to sin, because men do not believe in me; in regard to righteousness, because I am going to the Father, where you can see me no longer; and in regard to judgment, because the prince of this world now stands condemned" (John 16:8-11).

The Holy Spirit would convict the world in regard to righteousness because Jesus was going to the Father, and the disciples would see him no longer. Jesus' resurrection and ascension culminated his full work: his incarnation, his sinless life, his death and resurrection. Submitting to John for baptism marked the beginning of all he would do. He fulfilled all righteousness, beginning in baptism and ending in his ascension to the Father.

The Baptism of Believers

The third baptism is Christian baptism. The following passage, known as the Great Commission, must have a prominent place in our commitment to Christ.

> "Then Jesus came to them and said, 'All authority in heaven and on earth has been given to me. Therefore go and make disciples of all nations, baptizing them in the name of the Father and of the Son and of the Holy Spirit, and teaching them to obey everything I have commanded you. And surely I am with you always, to the very end of the age'" (Matthew 28:18-20).

T. C. Smith says, "John's baptism looked forward to an event in history that was to come. He called for repentance in baptism in anticipation of the new era. Christian baptism was a proclamation that the new era had arrived."[85]

The Greek word *baptizo* means to dip or to immerse.

> "As Jesus was **coming up out of the water**, he saw heaven being torn open and the Spirit descending on him like a dove" (Mark 1:10).

A rabbinic instruction for Jewish proselyte baptism advised the use of at least 100 gallons of water. For believers, baptism by immersion symbolizes the death, burial and resurrection of Jesus and the believer's identification with him in those acts. See Romans 6:1-6.

Baptism is not just a mechanical rite. In fact, in the New Testament accounts, baptism in water never preceded preaching, conviction, repentance and trust. Instead, the Scripture shows that when a person trusted Jesus, water baptism immediately followed. To be a Christian without baptism was unthinkable because the rite gave outward expression to an inward reality.

Because baptism indicated the embracing of a new way of life, leaving one lifestyle behind and embracing another, Paul often used the metaphor of baptism as a "putting off" and "putting on."

> "In him you were also circumcised, in the putting off of the sinful nature, not with a circumcision done by the hands of men but with the circumcision done by Christ, having been buried with him in baptism and raised with him through your faith in the power of God, who raised him from the dead" (Colossians 2:11-12).

> "Since, then, you have been raised with Christ, set your hearts on things above, where Christ is seated at the right hand of God... Do not lie to each other, since you have taken off your old self with its practices and have put on the new self, which is being renewed in knowledge in the image of its Creator" (Colossians 3:1, 9-10).

"Baptism is not the formation of new, isolated selves; it is rather the formation of a new people, the Body of Christ, by the power of the Spirit. As such, baptized believers are becoming holy by learning to live together as forgiven and forgiving people in mission to the world."[86] Baptism is public admission that a person is becoming incorporated into the family of God. The New Testament does not model hyper-individualism, which is a maverick Christianity.

THE LORD'S SUPPER

"They devoted themselves to the apostles' teaching and to the fellowship, to the breaking of bread and to prayer" (Acts 2:42).

Though the Greek meaning of "breaking of bread" could be eating together, the more common understanding among Bible scholars is that breaking of bread refers to what we call the Lord's Supper. Certainly in the Early Church, the two were not separated because believers had a fellowship meal along with the Lord's Supper. In the church at Corinth the "love feast" became greatly abused and received the rebuke in I Corinthians 11:17-29. (Please read this passage before continuing.)

Receiving the bread and the cup is an occasion for solemn self-examination, but not for morbid introspection. We can trust the promise of Scripture,

"If we confess our sins, he is faithful and just and will forgive us our sins and purify us from all unrighteousness" (I John 1:9).

The Lord's Supper is also a time of thanksgiving.

"Is not the cup of thanksgiving for which we give thanks a participation in the blood of Christ? And is not the bread that we break a participation in the body of Christ?" (I Corinthians 10:16).

The word "thanksgiving" in this verse is the Greek word *eucharistos*, and even today some traditions use the term

109

"Eucharist" instead of "the Lord's Supper." Thanksgiving and gratitude remain prominent elements of this observance.

There is an historical continuity between the Roman Catholic Church and the Early Church in the daily observance of the Eucharist. Even during the period when the priests, the pope and the political officials were corrupt, the believers still saw the cross of Christ every day in the observance of the Lord's Supper. Admittedly, "by the late Middle Ages regular partaking of the Supper became the sole prerogative of monks and priests, and only one annual Communion at Easter was expected of the people."[87] However, eventually the daily observance was restored.

Many Jewish scholars believe that during their long period of dispersion, the observance of the Sabbath preserved Jewish people as a distinct group. In the same way, it may be said that observance of the Lord's Supper did the same for the Christian church throughout history.

Despite varying views of what transpires at the Lord's table, believers can agree with Timothy George's statement: "If the Lord's Supper is given to us for 'daily food and sustenance to refresh and strengthen us' (Martin Luther), if it 'supports and augments faith' (Hulfrych Zwingli), if it is a 'spiritual banquet' (John Calvin) and the 'Christian marriage feast at which Jesus Christ is present with his grace, Spirit and promise' (Menno Simons), then to neglect its frequent sharing in the context of worship is to spurn the external sign of God's grace, to our spiritual impoverishment."[88]

I am convinced that many congregations should return to a more frequent observance of the Lord's Supper.

CHAPTER 5

CHURCH DISCIPLINE

Church Discipline is the continuing work of **discipleship**. We must recognize the connection between the two. Both come from the Latin word *discipulus*, meaning "learner." "It is the function of the church to disciple all nations and to discipline its own membership."[89]

"The Belgic Confession (1561), which grew out of Reformation soil, identifies three characteristics by which the true church is known. These marks are: (1) the preaching of pure doctrine, (2) the administering of the sacraments, and (3) the exercising of church discipline."[90]

The Westminster Confession of Faith, completed in 1646, affirms church discipline. "(It is) necessary for the reclaiming and gaining of offending brethren, for deterring of others from the like offences, for purging out of that leaven which might infect the whole lump, for vindicating the honour of Christ, and the holy profession of the gospel, and for preventing the wrath of God, which might justly fall upon the church, if they should suffer His covenant, and the seals thereof, to be profaned by notorious and obstinate offenders."[91]

"All of the great traditions at the core of American evangelicalism, whether the Reformed tradition, the Wesleyan Methodist tradition, or the Anabaptist tradition, understood church discipline when they were strong and thriving. But very few evangelical churches these days have any serious appropriation and practice of church discipline."[92]

"A viable and visible Church cannot – and should not – avoid the exercise of discipline."[93] To discipline is to provide treatment suited to a disciple or a learner, not to punish but to educate. Even when painful corrective measures are involved, discipline must be an exercise of love.

When done with legalistic, unloving attitudes, the practice goes beyond Scripture, which is why many churches have discontinued its use. An attitude of love, grace and humility must be evident at all times. Anything said or done that does not conform to the example and teaching of Jesus can be disastrous.

> "Brothers, if someone is caught in a sin, you who are spiritual should restore him gently. But watch yourself, or you also may be tempted" (Galatians 6:1).

God is our example in discipline, as indicated in Hebrews 12:5-11. If we love each other, we must be responsible to each other and exercise discipline in the church.

> "Those whom I love I rebuke and discipline. So be earnest, and repent" (Revelation 3:19).

The words "rebuke" and "chasten" are employed in the King James Version and the New King James Version of this verse. The Greek word *elegcho,* translated "rebuke," means to expose with a view to correction, and the Greek word translated "chasten" describes the discipline given to a child. Because the Greek *paideuo* means "chasten" and *pais* is the Greek word for "child," the original language referred to the discipline given a child in training or in "bringing him up."

The intention of biblical discipline is positive and redemptive, not negative or destructive. In fact, discipline is intended to induce repentance for the sake of eventual reconciliation, which is the ultimate goal.

In Matthew 18:15-17 Jesus gave the procedure for reconciliation and, if necessary, church discipline. When a need arises to follow these steps, those who administer the discipline must talk to the Lord first to make sure that no self-righteousness or pride is present and that the discipline is intended in the spirit of Jesus. Confession of their own sins to the Lord and requests for his cleansing are prerequisites. Then the procedure outlined in Matthew 18:15-17 can begin:

Step 1: Meet in private, "between the two of you" (verse 15). This should be a loving, caring conversation, with the desire to see the issue resolved at this point. If the offense is widely known, then some time after this private meeting, confession and repentance must be expressed by the offending person to the congregation.

Step 2: If the offender will not listen, meet with him with "one or two others along" (verse 16). Once again the hope is that the offender will "listen" and respond appropriately. These "witnesses" may well be elders in case additional steps are required.

Step 3: "If he refuses to listen to them, tell it to the church" (verse 17). At this point all the elders, as representatives of the church, should hear the full account and again appeal to the offender to acknowledge his sin, confess and repent before those present and to any others aware of the situation, whether a few persons or the entire congregation. If no repentance is evident, the elders present the case to the church in open forum and announce the offender's dismissal from church fellowship.

Step 4: "…If he refuses to listen even to the church, treat him as you would a pagan or tax collector" (verse 17). Though these words of the Lord seem harsh and vindictive, he did not contradict his own character and teaching. Certainly the attitude of Jesus would equal that of the Apostle Paul when he says, "Do not associate with him… Yet do not regard him as an enemy, but warn him as a brother" (II Thessalonians 3:14-15).

Pagans were considered persons void of good moral character. In New Testament times tax collectors were often corrupt and abusive in their collection methods, not persons Christians were to associate with habitually. The Apostle Paul warned, "Bad company corrupts good character" (I Corinthians 15:33). Yet, under the mandate of Christ, the early Christians longed to see pagans and tax collectors come to an enriching personal relationship with Jesus Christ. Today this same desire applies to the delinquent church member. The goal is always restoration and reconciliation.

Church discipline is essential not only for the good of the offender but also for the health of the Body. "People committed to living truthfully and also to living peaceably in communion cannot avoid the (regrettable) necessity of some forms of disciplinary – perhaps coercive – action. Minimally, such action is required as a way of clarifying through disciplined practices what are and are not appropriate attitudes, judgments, and behaviors within the community. Hence the importance of identifying those who are enemies of the truth, who refuse to participate honestly and faithfully in the deliberations about the good of the community's life. Every sustainable community must have boundaries; practices of forgiveness and reconciliation, and more specifically of loving enemies, are designed to prevent those boundaries from becoming barriers that wall the community off into a self-enclosed enclave."[94]

My experience with lovingly exercised scriptural discipline has always resulted in a positive outcome. Sometimes the result will be different because people choose to be resentful and rebellious. Yet, the only thing more difficult than obeying God is disobeying him. In the hope of clarifying this church practice, I offer two examples from my own experience.

A lady in our church bragged at every opportunity about how she mistreated her husband, boasting that she did not permit him to sleep with her but made him sleep in the basement. She often belittled him in the presence of others.

As her pastor, I and several elders confronted her about her destructive behavior. We appealed to her to confess her words and actions as sin and to repent.

Despite her initial resistance, she agreed to a time of prayer with us. The Holy Spirit softened her heart, and in tears she confessed her sin. She expressed the desire to do whatever was necessary to correct the situation.

She confessed to her husband and asked for his forgiveness. Because the situation was known throughout the church, we told her that she would need to confess before the congregation as well. We also required that she and her husband receive counseling.

They both readily agreed. The following Sunday at the end of the service they stood together before the congregation, confessed their sin, and asked for forgiveness, requesting the church's prayers and help.

She quoted Proverbs 14:1: "The wise woman builds her house, but with her own hands the foolish one tears hers down."

She said, "I have been a foolish woman, tearing my home apart." The husband confessed that he had not been the husband he should have been, especially in failing to be the spiritual leader in the home.

As pastor, I invited those who wished to pray with them to come forward. It seemed the entire congregation responded. The area around the altar was full, with people standing in the aisles.

Other husbands confessed that they had not been the spiritual leaders for their families. Wives expressed the desire to do their part in having godly homes. It was a glorious time together. God used this couple's public confession to bless the church greatly. Twenty-five years later the couple is still serving the Lord.

In another church that I served, a young man lived with a woman outside of marriage.

When the elders confronted him, he pledged to stay away from her. Instead, he kept returning to the relationship. Ultimately, he was dismissed from membership.

In this case, I felt that I should continue to meet with him and help him receive God's guidance. Eventually he broke off the illicit relationship and humbly received my mentoring. One year later, he was restored to fellowship. When I explained his spiritual maturation process, the congregation received him warmly. He went on to get training in biblical counseling and joined the church staff as a counselor. He now has a lovely family and is serving God faithfully. I wonder where he would be now if we had left him in his sin.

It is imperative that a list of sins which are subject to discipline be made available to every church member, perhaps in new member materials or in the church member handbook. Appendix 3 is a sample of such a list. Also, the goal of church discipline should be clearly stated.

Having the courage to exercise church discipline according to God's Word is an essential aspect of replicating and multiplying churches that disciple nations.

In addition to visible sins that may require church discipline, "silent sins" can greatly damage the fellowship of believers. Jesus mentioned "evil thought, greed, malice, envy and arrogance" (Mark 7:21-22). In the Apostle Paul's list of sins he included hatred, jealousy and selfish ambition, *i.e.* pride, (Galatians 5:20), along with the attitudes of heart that grieve the Holy Spirit (Ephesians 4:30) and put out the Spirit's fire (I Thessalonians 5:19). Sinful attitudes can prevent the Holy Spirit from accomplishing what God desires for his people. Such tragedy happens in many churches. "Man looks at the outward appearance, but the Lord looks at the heart" (I Samuel 16:7).

Constant intercessory prayer for the spiritual health of the Body and biblical instruction will combat these "silent enemies."

CHAPTER 6

SPIRITUAL GIFTS

"Now about spiritual gifts, brothers, I do not want you to be ignorant" (I Corinthians 12:1).

Because of Paul's clear statement, we cannot in good conscience ignore the subject of spiritual gifts. However, as with any other biblical doctrine, we must establish a final authority for our beliefs and actions.

Four possible sources can be considered:

Internal authorities: experience and reason

External authorities: the Church and the Bible.

We must settle forever that our final and supreme authority is the Bible itself.

The Holy Spirit inspired the Bible and he will never give us an experience contrary to what he inspired. The Holy Spirit is one in essence and nature with Jesus Christ and will never prompt us to do anything contrary to the character, conduct and compassion of Jesus.

We "know in part" (I Corinthians 13:12), a truth that should help us avoid two extreme views of spiritual gifts:

1. *Charis-mania*, an unbalanced and unscriptural emphasis on the gifts which distorts them out of biblical proportion

2. *Charis-phobia,* an unhealthy, persistent and illogical fear of spiritual gifts.

In view of our partial knowledge, every person speaking about spiritual gifts would do well to preface what he says with the statement, "as I understand the spiritual gifts." This humble admission is appropriate, without exception, no matter who is speaking. The Bible is not always explicit and exhaustive when it comes to spiritual gifts, which leaves room for sincere differences of opinion. Unpleasant experiences confirm that true "Bible-believing" Christians can hold diametrically opposed viewpoints. Such differences should not be tests of Christian fellowship.

The Importance of the Fruit of the Spirit

A discussion of spiritual gifts must acknowledge their relationship with the fruit of the Spirit. (See Galatians 5:22-23.) Spiritual gifts relate to what we *do*. The fruit of the Spirit relates to what we *are*.

Both fruit and gifts must be nurtured because both are absolutely essential and deserve equal attention and emphasis.

Fruit exhibits the characteristics of Christ which the Holy Spirit produces in us. Paul listed "love" first, probably because it manifests itself in the other fruit he listed:

> Joy, love's strength
> Peace, love's security
> Patience, love's endurance
> Kindness, love's conduct
> Goodness, love's character
> Faithfulness, love's confidence
> Gentleness, love's humility
> Self-control, love's victory.

"Against such things there is no law" (Galatians 5:23).

Unity and Maturity

The exercise of spiritual gifts apart from love does not produce **unity**. The Corinthian church did not lack any spiritual gift (I Corinthians 1:7); yet they were divided (I Corinthians 1:10-13).

The exercise of the spiritual gifts alone does not produce Christlike **maturity**. Those in the Corinthian church did not lack any spiritual gift, but they were spiritual babies (I Corinthians 3:1-3).

The statement in I Corinthians 14:1 sums up the scriptural balance:

"Pursue love, yet desire earnestly spiritual gifts" (NASB).

The Central Issue

The central issue in a believer's life is not spiritual gifts, but the Lordship of Jesus Christ (I Corinthians 12:3). The Holy Spirit's primary task is to give witness to Jesus and to give us the desire and power to respond to his authority (John 15:26; John 16:7-15). Though we must affirm and exercise our spiritual gifts, the primary emphasis is to be upon Jesus himself.

> "Once it was the blessing, now it is the Lord;
> Once it was the feeling, now it is His Word;
> Once His gift I wanted, now, the Giver own;
> Once I sought for healing, now Himself alone.
> All in all forever, Jesus will I sing;
> Everything in Jesus, and Jesus everything."
> ("Himself" by Dr. A.B. Simpson.)

The Indwelling Holy Spirit

The Holy Spirit is resident in every believer, fulfilling Jesus's promise in John 14:17: "...he lives with you and will be in you." In the passage of Romans 8:9-11, Paul stated four times that the Holy Spirit dwells in a believer. In I Corinthians 6:19 he stressed it again: "Do you not know that your body is a temple of the Holy Spirit, who is in you, whom you have received from God?"

Three scriptural commands relate to the Holy Spirit:

1. "Be filled with the Spirit" (Ephesians 5:18).

The indwelling of the Holy Spirit and the filling of the Holy Spirit are different. If they were identical, the command to be filled would not be necessary. The same verse warns the believer: "Do not get drunk on wine." To be drunk on wine is to be under the control of wine. To be filled with the Spirit does not refer to quantity, as to fill a container with water, but to be under the con-

119

trol of the Spirit, to be fully surrendered to the mastery of the Holy Spirit, embracing his full ministry.

The Greek verb, *plerousthe,* translated "be filled" has specific features:

A. It is plural, making the command for everyone.
B. It is passive, something to be done for us and not something we can do.
C. It is present tense, meaning a continuing action.

It would not press the meaning to say the command means "You all be continuously being filled with the Spirit."

2. "Do not put out the Spirit's fire" (I Thessalonians 5:19) can be literally translated, "Stop putting out the Spirit's fire."

Immediately following this command is the command, "Do not treat prophecies with contempt" (verse 20). It seems that the leadership at Thessalonica had prohibited the exercise of certain gifts, probably including prophecy, and had quenched (put out) the burning presence of the Holy Spirit, just the opposite of what Paul wrote to Timothy, "I remind you to fan into flame the gift of God..." (II Timothy 1:6).

3. "And do not grieve the Holy Spirit of God..." (Ephesians 4:30), literally in the Greek, "And stop grieving the Spirit, the Holy Spirit of God."

The verse begins with the word "and," linking it with the previous verse, which cautions us against "unwholesome talk" (verse 29). To speak unwholesome or worthless words is offensive to the holiness of the Spirit.

Paul instructed the Ephesians about a number of ways believers can either grieve or honor the Holy Spirit (Ephesians 4:25-5:2).

Don't lie. Speak truthfully (4:25).

Don't allow anger to make you sin (4:26-27).

Don't steal. Instead, do useful work (4:28).

Speak only wholesome words (4:29).

Do not grieve the Holy Spirit (4:30).

Get rid of bitterness, rage, anger, brawling, slander and

other forms of malice (4:31).
Be kind and forgiving (4:32).
Imitate Christ (5:1).
Live a life of love (5:2).

If we are not to grieve the Holy Spirit, every known sin should be acknowledged, forsaken and confessed because we have the faithful promise found in I John 1:9, "If we confess our sins, he is faithful and just and will forgive us our sins and purify us from all unrighteousness."

Spiritual Gifts Today

As I understand the spiritual gifts, they are to operate in the church today. There is no evidence within the Scriptures to suggest that spiritual gifts would cease at some time after the New Testament era.

As for church leaders, both elders and deacons, Paul made no reference to spiritual gifts, except that the elder should be "able to teach." Instead he wrote extensively about character traits (I Timothy 3:1-13; Titus 1:5-9). Please see "Character Qualities of Church Leaders,"Part Three, Chapter Two.

Observations to Keep in Mind

The New Testament teaches that every believer is assured at least one spiritual gift and perhaps more. "Now to each one the manifestation of the Spirit is given for the common good" (I Corinthians 12:7).

References to spiritual gifts are found in

Romans 12:3-8
I Corinthians 12-14
Ephesians 4:11-16
I Peter 4:10-11.

From these passages we can define a spiritual gift as a supernatural ability or capacity given by God to every believer for service and ministry to build up the church and individuals within it.

A spiritual gift is unearned and unmerited, a grace gift, as we see from the following Greek words, transliterated into English.

Charis – grace, the free unmerited favor of God towards the undeserving and ill-deserving. The initiative of God in giving us the gift of salvation and the gift of the desire and the power to do his will in living out his life upon the earth.

Charisma – gift, the grace of God made specific. The grace of God demonstrated in a particular way.

Charismata – gifts, the plural of gift. The word from which we get our English word "charismatic."

Larry Hart reminds us that "our unity is in the grace (*charis*) we have all received; our diversity is in the grace-gift(s) (*charisma*) we have each received."[95]

Spiritual gifts, properly understood and properly exercised, result in the unity of the Body of Christ in carrying out our Lord's commission upon the earth, "...so that there should be no division in the body, but that its parts should have equal concern for each other" (I Corinthians 12:25).

"Among the variety of God's gifts, some are natural abilities and character qualities sanctified, while others correspond to nothing that was previously seen in the person's life. That the gift is from the Holy Spirit is more evident in the latter case than in the former, but the reality is that all our capacities for expressing Christ are spiritual gifts. By means of them, Christ from his throne uses us as his hands, feet, and mouth, even his smile, and speaks, meets, loves, saves, and sustains... The test of whether you are exercising a spiritual gift is that people in the church feel the influence of Christ through what you say and do."[96]

God himself in the person of the Holy Spirit selects and assigns spiritual gifts (I Corinthians 12:11). We do not select our spiritual gifts.

In I Corinthians 12:14-27 Paul compares the variety of spiritual gifts to the parts of the human body. From his discussion we can conclude:

1. The lack of a particular function does not eliminate any part from full participation in the body (verses 15-16).
2. A body made of parts all with the identical function is absurd (verse 17).

122

3. If all the parts were the same, there would be no body (verses 18-19).
4. No part can exclude another part (verses 20-21).
5. Every part fulfills a necessary function and each part should be consciously recognized (verses 22-24).
6. God's design is cooperation and unity (verse 24).
7. The cohesion of the Body requires mutual care and concern on the part of the members. "If one part suffers, every part suffers with it; if one part is honored, every part rejoices with it" (verse 26).

Other passages offer even more insight:
1. Spiritual gifts are not just for the select few or the spiritually elite. "Now to each one the manifestation of the Spirit is given for the common good" (I Corinthians 12:7).
2. No member of Christ's Body should feel more important than another member of Christ's Body. "For by the grace given me I say to every one of you: Do not think of yourself more highly than you ought..." (Romans 12:3).
3. Not one of us can function effectively by himself or herself. Spiritual gifts are not designed for "lone rangers." The church as the Body of Christ excludes free-lance Christianity. "Each member belongs to all the others" (Romans 12:5).
4. We should naturally expect a variety and diversity of functions and viewpoints in the Body of Christ. "Just as each of us has one body with many members, and these members do not all have the same function..." (Romans 12:4).

Each spiritual gift has three dimensions:
1. The gift itself – "There are different kinds of gifts, but the same Spirit" (I Corinthians 12:4).
2. The sphere in which the gift is performed – "There are different kinds of service, but the same Lord" (I Corinthians 12:5).
3. The working (NIV), operations (KJV), effects (NAS) of the gift – "There are different kinds of working, but the

same God works all of them in all men" (I Corinthians 12:6). The Greek word transliterated is *energmaton.* The first five letters are the same as the English word energize. So the third dimension of the spiritual gift may be defined as energizing, operational power with its corresponding effect or result.

The one true God, as Father, Son and Holy Spirit, is involved in all three dimensions. From I Corinthians 12:4-6 we see that:

> The same God, the Holy Spirit, gives the gifts.
> The same God, the Lord Jesus Christ, assigns the ministry or service.
> The same God, the Father, turns on the energy.

Each gift has these three aspects, reminding us of the doctrine of the Trinity: We affirm one God who exists in his threefold nature as Father, Son and Holy Spirit, each with distinct personal attributes, but without division of nature, essence or being.

I believe that the Apostle Paul's lists of spiritual gifts are representative and not exhaustive. The gift of martyrdom may be suggested in I Corinthians 13:3; the gift of hospitality in I Peter 4:9-10; the gift of celibacy in I Corinthians 7:7, to name a few.

As we have seen previously in this chapter, every spiritual gift is strategic to the Body of Christ. Unfortunately, the gifts of healing, speaking in tongues and interpreting tongues, sometimes called the "sign-gifts," often receive more attention and in some circles are considered of greater value. Such a view is clearly unscriptural.

The Scripture lists spiritual gifts but does not define them. The Apostle Paul's discussions in I Corinthians 12 through 14 give insight into their meaning. In this same passage we find instructions on how the gifts are to be exercised, concluding, "everything should be done in a fitting and orderly way" (I Corinthians 14:40).

For the purposes of this book, I do not discuss each of the gifts. I mention only a few.

Prophecy

I appreciate Wayne Grudem's definition of prophecy:

"Although several definitions have been given for the gift of prophecy, a fresh examination of the New Testament teaching on this gift will show that it should be defined not as 'predicting the future,' nor as 'proclaiming a word from the Lord,' nor as 'powerful preaching' – but rather as 'telling something that God has spontaneously brought to mind.'"[97]

I would add that occasionally prophecy has to do with the future but most often it applies to the immediate situation. I Corinthians 14:3 states one result of authentic prophecy: "But everyone who prophesies speaks to men for their strengthening, encouragement and comfort."

Another result is the conviction of sin on the part of non-believers (I Corinthians 14:24). Please see more in the section "Prophet," in Part Three, Chapter Three.

Faith

Often the question is asked, "If every Christian is supposed to have faith, what is the gift of faith?" I believe it is the special ability God gives some believers to demonstrate extraordinary confidence in God and his promises. This is a pioneering, "out front" kind of faith distinct from the measure of faith most Christians experience which is essential to salvation and service.

Healing

The way God works in physical healing is a considerable mystery. It is of interest that this gift is expressed in the plural, "gifts of healings" (I Corinthians 12:9, 28), allowing room for some inferences:

1. There are varieties of healings for varieties of illnesses: physical, mental, spiritual.
2. God does not turn men into healers. God himself heals through human agents as he gives "gifts of healings,"

focusing our attention upon God who heals and not upon the agents he chooses to use. In contrast to references to "prophets," "teachers," and "evangelists," the Bible never refers to men as "healers."

3. God seems to concentrate his "gifts of healings" in certain individuals at certain times more than in others. They always remain God's gifts and are never under the control of man to be manipulated at will. At times persons not at all known for healing ministries will themselves manifest God's "gifts of healings."

James 5:13-16 attests that healing should be a part of the church's ministry. God, who is complete love and who has complete knowledge, exercises his freedom in the area of healing. By faith we should expect him to heal but we should never demand that he heal.

It is important to recognize that God heals in different ways:
1. Instantly and directly
2. Gradually through natural processes
3. Through medical science

God also gives grace to suffer by healing attitudes and emotions. For the Christian, God may use death as the ultimate healing.

Members of my family have received medically certified instant healing as a result of prayer with only one person or a few persons present. On the other hand, I have witnessed a prayer vigil of people at the church altar around the clock for a week, praying for the healing of a child. And yet the child died.

In Deuteronomy we read:

"The secret things belong to the Lord our God, but the things revealed belong to us and to our children forever, that we may follow all the words of this law"
(Deuteronomy 29:29).

In the matter of healing, there are some things God has chosen not to reveal. In faith, I have come to be content with this, based on the scriptural truth that God is good and what he does is good. Also, in faith, I pray for the healing of others. I believe God's statement to Moses, speaking of the Israelites, "I am the Lord who heals you" (Exodus 15:26).

Tongues

If we can accept the proposition that all the gifts are operational today, we should expect some Christians to speak in tongues. Paul gives instructions for their use in public (I Corinthians 14). Following these guidelines will eliminate most of the problems concerning tongues. It is the abuse of tongues and not the use of tongues that has caused a negative response on the part of many.

Miracles

Another gift listed in the plural is "miraculous powers," literally workings or operations of powers (I Corinthians 12:10). This is the manifestation of the Holy Spirit at various times through the agency of believing Christians to perform powerful acts that alter what is perceived to be the ordinary course of nature, *i.e.*, dramatic demonstrations of God's absolute control over all created beings and things. This gift is sometimes associated with casting out demons. See Mark 9:38-39 as one example.

Love Must Remain Central

There is divine purpose in Paul's decision to place the love chapter (I Corinthians 13) directly in the center of his discussion of the gifts. And in Romans 12, after listing a number of spiritual gifts, Paul spent the balance of the chapter, verses 9-21, describing how love acts. It is God's intention that all spiritual gifts be exercised in love and humility. Without love and humility much confusion can result.

Again, we need to remember the admonition of I Corinthians 14:40: "Everything should be done in a fitting and orderly way." Jack Hayford points out that "the word 'charming' would not be an inappropriate translation of the word 'fitting' (decently). 'Let things be done in a graceful and charming way.'"[98]

Identifying Spiritual Gifts

A brief book by Bruce Bugbee is an excellent source to use in identifying one's spiritual gift(s). He suggests that we consider spiritual gifts in the context of God-given passion and personal style. I owe much of the following to his book.[99]

God-given Passion

In discussing God-given passion Bugbee asks, "What do you care about the most? For what do you have a passion? Where would you like to see your life make a difference?" He defines a God-given **passion** as the God-given desire of the heart to make a difference somewhere, to glorify God and edify people.

He discusses three types of **passion**:

1. People-passion longs to make a difference in the lives of people.
2. Function-passion desires to be involved in projects and tasks that serve people and advance the cause of Christ.
3. Cause-passion is highly motivated to address certain causes, for example, evangelism, prayer, world missions, world hunger, human rights and stewardship of the environment. The cause-driven person is eager to enlist others in the cause.

Questions to ask yourself: "Am I doing anything about my heart's desire? Am I fulfilling my passion and finding fulfillment?"

Personal Style

Bugbee describes **personal style**, also referred to as personality or temperament, as the way you prefer to relate to the world around you, your most natural way of relating to others. "Your personal style is unique to you, and it energizes you. There are some kinds of activities that give us energy and some that seem to take energy from us."[100]

You may be people-oriented or task-oriented, structured or unstructured. Usually we are not entirely one or the other, but are one primarily and the other secondarily. The question is, "If there were no consequences to the way you organized your relationships and life, which would you be?"

We are most comfortable and more energized when we are operating within our personal style. "When we move consistently further away from our personal style preferences, boredom or burnout results."[101]

Additional Suggestions

In addition to Bugbee's comments, I would like to suggest other practical ways you can explore your spiritual gifts. Get involved in service and ministry. Once you are involved in various ministries, examine your feelings. Determine which produces excitement and gratification. Evaluate the results.

Spiritual gifts produce observable spiritual results. For example, if you feel that you have the gift of teaching, at least two things should happen: Christians should gravitate to you as a teacher, and there should be evidence of life-changing spiritual results. Remain alert to the responses of other Christians because your gifts should be confirmed by the Body of Christ.

Undue Focus on Spiritual Gifts

Some words of caution: Excessive emphasis on spiritual gifts can produce negative results. Sincere Christians can become so preoccupied with their efforts to "pigeonhole" their spiritual gifts that frustration blurs their vision of Christ and diminishes their relationship to him. The primary emphasis should be on the Giver, who is Jesus Christ the Lord.

Some who feel they have affirmed their spiritual gifts rationalize their failure to serve in other areas of need with the excuse, "That is not my spiritual gift."

Spiritual pride develops quickly when there is excessive emphasis on spiritual gifts. God actively opposes pride. The Scripture admonishes believers to "desire spiritual gifts" for the church (I Corinthians 14:1); but nowhere in the Bible do we find any exhortation for individual Christians "to search for" or "try to discover" spiritual gifts. Apparently in the New Testament the spiritual gifts became evident in due course as Christians loved and served Jesus and loved and served others. A compulsive searching for spiritual gifts is not evident in Scripture. Sensitivity to the guidance of the Holy Spirit, as he leads you to be obedient to Christ, will prevent excess in seeking to identify your gift(s).

"Paul told the Corinthians to seek the best gifts. Other things being equal, the best gifts will always be those that express the most love and do most good to most people."[102]

To this point, the gifts discussed are those given to individual believers to strengthen the church. In a later section we will consider the "equipping ministries" of apostles, prophets, evangelists, pastors and teachers (Ephesians 4:11).

Baptism with the Holy Spirit

Because this subject is the cause of much interest and often much disagreement, a discussion is included here.

The phrases "baptism with the Holy Spirit" or "baptism of the Holy Spirit" are not found in Scripture. The verb "baptize" is used, apparently to denote the action of the Holy Spirit rather than a static event. The term comes from John the Baptist:

> "I would not have known him, except that the one who sent me to baptize with water told me, 'The man on whom you see the Spirit come down and remain is he who will baptize with the Holy Spirit'" (John 1:33).

This statement by John the Baptist is also recorded in the Synoptic Gospels in Matthew 3:11, Mark 1:8 and Luke 3:16.

Jesus referred to John the Baptist's statement in Acts 1:5, and in Acts 11:16 Peter repeated Jesus' words. These references are the only New Testament verses which use the phrase "baptize with the Holy Spirit." At Pentecost and afterward the term is not used.

Luke described the experience at Pentecost as being *filled* with the Holy Spirit."

"All of them were filled with the Holy Spirit and began to speak in other tongues as the Spirit enabled them" (Acts 2:4).

As Peter addressed the crowd in Acts 4:8-12 he was "filled with the Holy Spirit" (verse 8).

Describing the event in Cornelius' house, Luke said, "The Holy Spirit came... The Holy Spirit had been poured out... " and "They have received" (Acts 10:44-47).

In Acts 15, before the council in Jerusalem, Peter reported, "God, who knows the heart, showed that he accepted them by giving the Holy Spirit to them, just as he did to us" (Acts 15:8).

"The Scripture offers us sufficient variety so that we need not make mere terminology a matter of offense or misunderstanding."[103]

Different Opinions

A number of views have arisen concerning the baptism of the Holy Spirit.

North American classical Pentecostalism speaks in terms of a "second experience," subsequent to salvation with the initial evidence of speaking in tongues.

Others, like J. Rodman Williams and Arnold Bittlinger, believe that baptism of the Holy Spirit accompanies baptism with water and is later appropriated (Williams) or released (Bittlinger), an idea like the formal view of North American Roman Catholic charismatics, who strongly deny a "second work of grace." (In general, however, views among Catholic laity vary on this subject.)

Peter Wagner, who has awakened traditional North American denominations to an awareness of spiritual gifts, uses the term "third wave" to indicate that all the gifts are operational today. The group agreeing with Wagner endorses the concept of baptism with the Holy Spirit which may or may not involve speaking in tongues.

May All Speak In Tongues?

May all speak in tongues? This question causes much debate. Some answer, "Yes, all the people did the day the church was born at Pentecost. If all then, why not all now?"

One view about the observers' experience at Pentecost is that it resulted from a "miracle of hearing" (Acts 2:6). Further, this view holds that the tongues referred to in I Corinthians 12 and 14 are the same as those at Pentecost.

A different opinion is held by those who insist that the tongues at Pentecost were actually many different human languages.

The Apostle Paul asked, "Do all have gifts of healing? Do all speak in tongues? Do all interpret?" (I Corinthians 12:30).

1. The Greek language construct requires the answer, "No," with the inferred conclusion that not all believers may speak in tongues.

2. Some argue that these questions refer to "tongues for the public assembly" and not to tongues "as a personal prayer language." The term *prayer language* emerges from the Apostle Paul's statement, "I thank God that I speak in tongues more than all of you. But in the church I would rather speak five intelligible words to instruct others than ten thousand words in a tongue" (I Corinthians 14:18-19).

The problem with these varied perceptions of tongues is that exactly the same Greek word is used in every case.

The following is a sincere, if humorous, comment by Jack Hayford, long-time pastor of Church on the Way, Van Nuys, California:

"Some say that if you don't speak in tongues you are not filled with the Holy Spirit. A long time ago I decided that it's not my business to tell people if they're filled with the Spirit, whether they speak with tongues or not. God knows if they're filled with the Spirit and it's not my business to label them. I rejected, 'if you don't then you aren't.' One reason I knew that was not true was because I'd seen a lot of people who 'did and weren't.'"[104] Hayford believes that every believer may speak in tongues and speaks strongly of the blessing of speaking in tongues.

"It is evident that no clear-cut theological formulation of this phenomenon [the baptism with the Holy Spirit] has yet emerged in the charismatic movement. What we have at present is a variety of ways for describing and explaining what is the same essential reality or experience."[105]

When we differ in our understanding of the baptism of the Holy Spirit, we should act in grace with one another. We need to remember the words of Oswald Chambers, "It takes God a long time to get us to stop thinking that unless everyone sees things exactly as we do, they must be wrong."[106]

PART THREE

Leaders of the Church

Chapter One: The Functions of Leaders

Chapter Two: The Character Qualities of Leaders

Chapter Three: Leaders as Equippers

CHAPTER 1

THE FUNCTIONS OF LEADERS

The terms shepherd (pastor), overseer (bishop) and elder in Scripture apply interchangeably to the same persons.

"From Melitus, Paul sent to Ephesus for the elders of the church" (Acts 20:17).

"Keep watch over yourselves and all the flock of which the Holy Spirit has made you overseers. Be shepherds of the church of God, which he bought with his own blood" (Acts 20:28).

"To the elders among you... Be shepherds of God's flock that is under your care, serving as overseers..."
(I Peter 5:1-2).

"Shepherd" and "overseer" describe functions, while "elder" appears to be a title of honor and respect. The word "pastor" occurs only once in the English language New Testament (Ephesians 4:11). The same Greek word is translated "shepherd" in all other verses.

Shepherd (Pastor)

Psalm 23 and John 10 describe some of the functions of the "Good Shepherd," the Lord Jesus. Parallels appear in the ministry of the under-shepherd (pastor).

He feeds the flock.

"...I shall not be in want... You prepare a table before me..." (Psalm 23:1, 5).

137

"He will come in and go out, and find pasture" (John 10:9).

He seeks to provide an environment conducive to spiritual growth.
"He guides me in paths of righteousness for his name's sake" (Psalm 23:3).

He attends to the hurts and special needs of the flock.
"He makes me lie down in green pastures, he leads me beside quiet waters, he restores my soul... You anoint my head with oil; my cup overflows" (Psalm 23:2, 5).

He walks with the flock through hard places.
"Even though I walk through the valley of the shadow of death, I will fear no evil, for you are with me... " (Psalm 23:4).

He comforts the flock.
"...your rod and your staff, they comfort me" (Psalm 23:4).

He lays down his life for the flock.
"I am the good shepherd. The good shepherd lays down his life for the sheep" (John 10:11).

Besides Psalm 23 and John 10, other Scriptures describe the functions of the pastor, for instance **he is to pray for the sick when requested:**

"...call the elders of the church to pray over him and anoint him with oil in the name of the Lord" (James 5:14).

The book of Acts demonstrates that **shepherd duties include protecting the flock from all kinds of danger:**
The danger of unregenerate men getting into the fellowship and causing damage and destruction:

"...savage wolves will come in among you and will not spare the flock..." (Acts 20:29).

The danger of men within the fellowship seeking to establish parties and divisions:

"Even from your own number men will arise and distort the truth in order to draw away disciples after them" (Acts 20:30).

The danger of false doctrine:
Please read the lengthy passage in Acts 15:4-29.

Overseer (Bishop)

The Greek word for overseer (*bishop,* KJV) is *episkopos*, which combines *epi* (over) and *scopos* (watcher). So an overseer is a "watcher over." He is one who leads with authority, as the writer of Hebrews suggests:

> "Obey your leaders and submit to their authority. They keep watch over you as men who must give an account. Obey them so that their work will be a joy, not a burden, for that would be of no advantage to you" (Hebrews 13:17).

> "...Respect those who work hard among you, who are over you in the Lord. Hold them in the highest regard in love because of their work..." (I Thessalonians 5:12-13).

Authority can be abused, but rightly understood and appropriately applied, authority is divinely delegated for man's good. Clearly, believers are to obey their spiritual leaders and submit to their authority in the context of mutual submission, a parallel to the principle of submission within the family (Ephesians 5:21).

The authority of the "overseer" is always exercised in the context of the priesthood of all believers.

> "But you are a chosen people, a royal priesthood, a holy nation, a people belonging to God..." (I Peter 2:9).

The Greek word *laos*, translated "people," is the word from which the English word "laity" comes. No member of the church is excluded or exempted from the twofold ministry of intercession and witness: of intercession as priests for men before God, and of witness as priests for God before men.

This doctrine stands in contrast to the Roman Catholic position that certain ministries are exclusively the function of ordained priests. As we saw in the study of spiritual gifts, every member of the Body of Christ is strategic and significant.

Cults bearing the name "Christian" often insist that the "elders" direct, without question, every detail of the follower's life. The Scripture declares,

> "For there is one God and one mediator between God and men, the man Christ Jesus..." (I Timothy 2:5).

Therefore, the scriptural command to obey and submit to the overseers is to be done graciously but responsibly, testing everything by the self-evident truth of scripture.

Elder

Two categories of elders are referred to in I Timothy 5:17: **those who rule (KJV), direct affairs or administer** and **those who perform the same duties but also preach and teach.**

> "The elders who direct the affairs of the church well are worthy of double honor, especially those whose work is preaching and teaching."

Chapter 15 of Acts illustrates that **elders are to deal with and mediate disagreements among believers.**

Another duty is to **encourage believers to carry out Christ's instructions for settling personal disputes and for handling church discipline.**

> "Therefore, if you are offering your gift at the altar and there remember that your brother has something against you, leave your gift there in front of the altar. First go and be reconciled to your brother; then come and offer your gift" (Matthew 5:23-24).

The matter of church discipline from Matthew 18:15-17 is dealt with at length in the section on Church Discipline in Part

Two, Chapter Five. The dual objectives of settling personal disputes and exercising church discipline are

1. To maintain the health of the Body of Christ
2. To restore the offender.

The New Testament makes it evident that there was a plurality of elders, as already mentioned in Acts 20:17 and as shown in the following verses:

"...Appoint elders in every town, as I directed you" (Titus 1:5).

"...To the elders among you..." (I Peter 5:1).

The following chapter addresses the kind of person a church leader is to be.

PART THREE
LEADERS OF THE CHURCH

CHAPTER 2

THE CHARACTER QUALITIES OF LEADERS

(Based on I Timothy 3:1-7 and Titus 1:5-9)

1. ABOVE REPROACH (NIV, NASB), BLAMELESS (KJV) –
   Titus 1:7, I Timothy 3:2
   The Greek word *anepileptos* literally means "one who cannot be laid hold upon." Titus 1:7 uses a different Greek word *anegkletos* literally "one against whom it is impossible to bring a charge of wrongdoing." After objective and thorough examination, one against whom there is no scriptural basis for making an accusation.

2. THE HUSBAND OF ONE WIFE – I Timothy 3:2, Titus 1:6
   Literally "a man of one woman," totally and exclusively devoted to his wife.

3. TEMPERATE (NIV, NASB), VIGILANT (KJV) –
   I Timothy 3:2
   One who is usually moderate in thought, speech and behavior. One who is on guard against excess.

4. SELF-CONTROLLED (NIV), PRUDENT (NASB), SOBER (KJV) – I Timothy 3:2, SENSIBLE (NASB) — Titus 1:8
   One who is sensible, wise, balanced in judgment, not given to quick, superficial decisions based on immature thinking. Having common sense, not given to impulsiveness.

5. RESPECTABLE (NIV, NASB), OF GOOD BEHAVIOR (KJV) – I Timothy 3:2

The word *kosmios* could be translated "of orderly behavior" because it speaks of order as distinct from disorder, one who demonstrates a well-ordered life. In the Christian context, it speaks of a life integrated around the Lordship of Jesus Christ.

6. HOSPITABLE (NIV, NASB), GIVEN TO HOSPITALITY (KJV) – I Timothy 3:2

Literally "lover of strangers and foreigners." One who is open and loving toward those who are different from him.

7. NOT GIVEN TO DRUNKENNESS (NIV), NOT ADDICTED TO WINE (NASB), NOT GIVEN TO WINE (KJV) – I Timothy 3:3

Literally "Does not sit long at his wine." The biblical standard is moderation. Since one out of nine persons who ever takes a drink becomes either a problem drinker or an alcoholic, the only guarantee of moderation is total abstinence. Compare Romans 14:21.

In this regard, Bill Gothard has said, "What you allow in moderation, your children will excuse in excess." Also see Proverbs 20:1; 23:29-35.

8. NOT VIOLENT (NIV), NOT PUGNACIOUS (NASB), NO STRIKER (KJV) – I Timothy 3:3

Not eager to strike out at others. One who is characterized by forbearance, not quick-tempered.

9. NOT QUARRELSOME (NIV), NOT CONTENTIOUS (NASB), NOT A BRAWLER (KJV) – I Timothy 3:3

One not given to quarreling and argumentation. One who does not carry a chip on his shoulder. One who does not get his feelings hurt easily and frequently. Not one who causes others to be on guard about what they say or do for fear of offending him.

10. GENTLE (NIV, NASB), PATIENT (KJV) – I Timothy 3:3
Not unduly rigorous. Not making a determined and stubborn stand for one's just due and legal rights. Characterized by flexibility, a forbearing spirit, "sweet reasonableness." See Philippians 4:5, which uses the noun form of the same Greek word.

11. ONE WHO EFFECTIVELY CONTROLS HIS HOUSEHOLD, ESPECIALLY HIS CHILDREN – I Timothy 3:4-5, Titus 1:6
One who has a well-ordered household, a healthy family life and well-behaved children. A man whose children believe and are not open to the charge of being wild and disobedient. This requirement is generally understood to pertain to those children still under the authority of the parents.

12. NOT OVERBEARING (NIV), NOT SELF-WILLED (NASB, KJV) – Titus 1:7
Literally "not pleasing himself." One who is not eager to have his own way. Not one who obstinately maintains his own opinion or asserts his rights while indifferent to the rights, opinions and interests of others.

13. NOT QUICK-TEMPERED (NIV, NASB), NOT SOON ANGRY (KJV) – Titus 1:7
In the Greek, *me orgilon*. The word *orgilon* comes from the Greek word *orge*, which speaks of sustained, deliberately nurtured anger as contrasted to the Greek word *thumos,* an anger that quickly blazes up and quickly subsides. This kind of man is not quick-tempered and does not have a set disposition to anger. He is not an angry person. Also see Proverbs 22:24; 29:22; James 1:19-20.

14. DISCIPLINED (NIV), SELF-CONTROLLED (NASB), TEMPERATE (KJV) – Titus 1:8

Literally "having power over one's self." Characterized by self-discipline.

15. NOT A LOVER OF MONEY (NIV), FREE FROM THE LOVE OF MONEY (NASB), NOT GREEDY OF FILTHY LUCRE (KJV) – I Timothy 3:3, NOT PURSUING DISHONEST GAIN (NIV) – Titus 1:7

One who is not characterized by greed and unbalanced interest in material matters and financial gain. One who does not have a wrong value system. Jesus taught us to love persons and use things. A wrong value system causes us to love things and use persons.

16. NOT A RECENT CONVERT (NIV), NOT A NOVICE (KJV), NOT A NEW CONVERT (NASB) – I Timothy 3:6

Not a beginner in the Christian faith. A person may have been a Christian for many years and yet be a beginner in the things of the Lord. The servant leader must be a mature Christian. Read the entire verse: I Timothy 3:6.

17. HE MUST HAVE A GOOD REPUTATION WITH OUTSIDERS (NIV), HE MUST HAVE A GOOD REPUTATION WITH THOSE OUTSIDE THE CHURCH (NASB), HE MUST HAVE A GOOD REPORT OF THEM WHICH ARE WITHOUT (KJV) – I Timothy 3:7

The Greek word *kalos,* translated "good," speaks of good quality. The word translated "reputation" or "report" is the Greek word *marturian,* and means "a testimony in court or judicial evidence." So "good report" means good quality of testimony that can stand close examination in court, or "good judicial evidence." If this type man were "put on trial" for being a mature and dedicated follower of Jesus, there would be enough solid evidence to convict him. Please see I Thessalonians 4:11-12 and Colossians 4:5-6.

The Greek word *marturian* is the basis for our English word "martyr." Christians had convictions (testimonies) that caused them to remain faithful to Jesus even when it meant certain death. Because of the frequent civil trials of Christians who refused to abandon their faith, *marturian*, meaning "court testimony" came to be equated with death, thus *martyr*.

A leader of the church holds convictions for which he is willing to die rather than deny. Such non-negotiable convictions must be based on abundantly clear, self-evident interpretations of Scripture and not on any "private interpretation" subject to debate among Bible-believing Christians. Also see I Peter 3:15-17.

18. UPRIGHT (NIV), JUST (NASB, KJV) – Titus 1:8

The Greek word *dikaion*, which is translated here as "upright, just," is elsewhere often translated "righteous."

The just man has been put in right relationship with God by receiving Jesus as Lord and Savior. He has been declared "not guilty." As a result, the just man acts justly, rightly and is rightly related to others.

He has a clear conscience and can turn 360 degrees without seeing a person who can point an accusing finger at him and say, "You offended me, you did me wrong, and you did not do everything possible to make it right."

This man seeks in all things and in all relationships to do what is fair, just and right in God's sight. Also see Micah 6:8.

19. ONE WHO LOVES WHAT IS GOOD (NIV), A LOVER OF GOOD MEN (KJV), LOVING WHAT IS GOOD (NASB) – Titus 1:8

One who is an ally and enthusiastic supporter of the good, including persons, deeds, and things.

20. HOLY (NIV, KJV), DEVOUT (NASB) – Titus 1:8

One who is morally pure, characterized by moral excellence. One of unassailable character who devotedly seeks to live in harmony with God and God's will. One who is careful of his duties toward God and toward man, whose life reflects positively the character and reputation of God.

21. INTENSELY LOYAL TO THE REVEALED WORD OF GOD AS BEING COMPLETELY TRUSTWORTHY AND AUTHORITATIVE. AND ABLE TO TEACH IT BY PRECEPT AND EXAMPLE, IN ORDER TO ENCOURAGE BELIEVERS AND TO CONVICT OR CONVINCE UNBELIEVERS WHO CONTRADICT THE FAITH
This is a paraphrase of Titus 1:9. Please read it now. Also, read I Timothy 3:2 for another use of "able to teach."

CHAPTER 3

LEADERS AS EQUIPPERS

"It was he who gave some to be apostles, some to be prophets, some to be evangelists, and some to be pastors and teachers, to prepare God's people for works of service so that the body of Christ may be built up..." (Ephesians 4:11-12).

The Greek word *katartizo* translated "to prepare" literally means "to equip." Thus, in the New Revised Standard Version of the Bible this verse reads, "...to equip the saints for the work of ministry... " In non-biblical writing the word was used in reference to rigging out a ship to assure that it had everything necessary to be completely seaworthy, lacking nothing essential to a successful voyage.

The parallel to these equipping leaders is obvious: With God's help, they are to do everything possible to equip God's people so that they will be adequate and effective in doing the works of service.

Apostle

Some insist that the ministry of the apostle ended with the original twelve apostles. The usual comment is, "The apostle and prophets had a foundational ministry and they are not needed today." But in fact, at least nineteen apostles are designated by name in the New Testament. In I Corinthians 15 where Paul cited the resurrection appearances of Jesus, he said Jesus appeared to Peter, then to the Twelve, then to five hundred, then to James, then to all the apostles... (verses 5-7).

"Some have argued that apostles no longer exist today but this conclusion runs counter to Biblical evidence... Nothing in Paul's treatment of spiritual gifts suggests that he was describing a pattern for the Early Church only. Quite the opposite. For Paul the church is a growing, grace-filled body, and apostles are a permanent part of that body's life."[107]

What is the ministry of the apostle? The Greek word literally means "one who is sent." It came to have the weight of **an accredited representative with a commissioned authority**. Paul called himself "an apostle of Christ Jesus by the will of God" (I Corinthians 1:1). He stated that apostleship is anchored in servanthood (Romans 1:1). We see from Paul's ministry that apostles are gifted in establishing new groups of believers and building them up in the faith, as well as gifted in ministering to existing churches.

God uses the apostle to give foundational truth. "There is no new truth to be added to the Scriptures. The body of truth we have is to be taken by those who have the apostolic gift and imparted to new churches."[108] The apostle is also used to bring foundational truth to existing churches in their ongoing development.

An example of apostolic function is found in Paul's words to Titus in Titus 1:5, "I left you behind in Crete for this reason, so that you should put in order what remained to be done, and should appoint elders in every town..." (NRSV).

The apostle is not a free lancer floating around in a personal ministry apart from accountability to a local church. After Paul and Barnabas' first missionary journey, they reported to the "sending church," the church at Antioch (Acts 14:27). In addition, Paul spent three years in Ephesus living out the life of Jesus before the people and always remained accountable to the churches.

In one sense, today's missionary who preaches the Gospel and plants and nurtures churches may be called an apostle. In fact, both the word "apostle" from Greek and "missionary" from Latin mean "one who is sent."

Prophet

The Greek word *propheteuo* translated "to prophesy" literally means "to speak out." The prophet is the *out-speaker*. He primarily addresses the current need of God's people and less frequently predicts the future.

"He speaks out the counsel of God with the clearness, energy and authority which spring from the consciousness of speaking in God's name, and having a direct message from him to deliver."[109]

"The New Testament concept of a prophet was clearly based upon the Old Testament prophetic ministry, and included declaring God's Word, having supernormal knowledge, and evidencing the power of God."[110]

A casual reading of the books of Isaiah, Jeremiah, Amos and the other prophets reveals a number of characteristics of the prophet:

1. Sensitivity to God's standards and any deviation from or violation of them
2. A concern for God's reputation
3. A special capacity to hate evil, while showing compassion toward people
4. A directness, frankness and persuasiveness in speaking
5. A willingness to go through whatever it takes to see God's will accomplished, even criticism, heartache, grief and brokenness
6. A commitment to bring hope and restoration to those who correct their ways and turn to God in humility and trust.

Results determine the authenticity of a prophet's message. If he tells of future events, those events should transpire as predicted. I Corinthians 14:3 tells what some of the results should be in the lives of believers: "Everyone who prophesies speaks to men for their strengthening, *i.e.*, up building, encouragement, help, comfort and consolation" (my translation based on the subtleties of Greek word meanings).

In addition to the ministry to Christians, the prophet's message should bring conviction of sin and the response of faith and worship on the part of non-believers.

"But if an unbeliever or someone who does not understand comes in while everybody is prophesying, he will be convinced by all that he is a sinner and will be judged by all, and the secrets of his heart will be laid bare. So he will fall down and worship God, exclaiming, 'God is really among you!'" (I Corinthians 14:24-25).

The prophet willingly allows another to "weigh carefully what is said" (I Corinthians 14:29). The people who hear the prophet are to test his message.

"Dear friends, do not believe every spirit, but test the spirits to see whether they are from God, because many false prophets have gone out into the world" (I John 4:1).

Let me suggest three tests.
1. The love test. Can we see and hear the love of Jesus in the man and his message?
2. The character or moral test. Someone has said, "The prophet is not to traffic in unlived truths."
3. The scriptural or theological test. Does it pass the scrutiny of biblical truth? Does it contradict Scripture?

We are to follow the example of the Bereans.

"Now the Bereans were of more noble character than the Thessalonians for they received the message with great eagerness and examined the Scriptures every day to see if what Paul said was true" (Acts 17:11).

Evangelist

Evangelists are a part of the "equipping ministry" of the church. Every Christian is commissioned to engage in evangelism, to share the gospel with those who have not yet come to faith in Christ as Savior and Lord. The evangelist does more than tell the Good News to the unconverted; he equips and motivates the church to become evangelistic in lifestyle and also trains those who are gifted as evangelists.

152

The late Bill Bright was a prominent modern example of a biblical evangelist. He constantly witnessed one-on-one, but also challenged and equipped thousands to "do the work of an evangelist" (II Timothy 4:5).

Pastor/Teacher

The Greek grammatical construction indicates that the words "pastor" and "teacher" refer to one individual, *i.e.* one office with a dual function. The words "some to be" appear before every ministry except that of teacher. So the two words apply to one person. For translators this is called "Granvill Sharp's Rule."

Everything said previously in this book concerning pastors and teaching applies here.

To say that the pastor is also teacher does not suggest that he is the only one who teaches. Many Christians have the spiritual gift of teaching and should be fully released in the Body of Christ.

The Leadership Team

From Ephesians 4:11 we have what may be called the "Leadership Team," men who are each based in a local church, who labor together in ministering there and to the Church at large. They establish new churches and oversee the spiritual development of existing churches.

The usefulness of these special ministries given to the church is as great or as small as their effectiveness in developing mature Christians with fruitful ministries in the church and in their other areas of influence. After listing the equipping ministries, Paul states their purpose:

> "...so that the body of Christ may be built up until we all reach unity in the faith and in the knowledge of the Son of God and become mature, attaining to the whole measure of the fullness of Christ" (Ephesians 4:12-13).

If spiritual gifts distributed to all believers can be compared to the motor of a car then these gifted men are the steering wheel to guide it. A car with a motor and no steering wheel is dangerous. A car with a steering wheel and no motor is useless. Motor and steering wheel belong together. The spiritual gifts and the gifted men of Ephesians 4:11 belong together.[111]

PART FOUR

The Church Yesterday and Today

CHAPTER 1

THE MISSION OF THE CHURCH

The mission of the church is
To Glorify God
To Proclaim God's Message
To Disciple Believers

To Glorify God

The overreaching mission of the church is to glorify God. This is the theme of the letter to the Ephesians. The late W. T. Conner wrote a commentary on Ephesians entitled *The Glory of God in the Christian Calling.* I would change the title to *The Glory of God in the Calling of the Church.* The key verse of Ephesians is chapter 3, verse 21:

"...to him be glory in the church and in Christ Jesus throughout all generations, for ever and ever! Amen."

The very next verse, 4:1, challenges the Ephesians and us "...to live a life worthy of the calling you have received." Because the Greek text had no chapter and verse divisions, 3:21 and 4:1 were together. Unfortunately, our English translations separate them.

The glory of God is all that God is, made manifest. "The calling of the church is to reveal in the world the glory of God's character which is found in the person of Jesus Christ."[112] What does this statement mean for me? God's ultimate purpose for me is that his son Jesus Christ might be exhibited in me, a purpose that is true for every Christian.

Chapters four, five and six of Ephesians give Paul's detailed description of how this may be done. Please read these chapters carefully and prayerfully.

When we read the biblical challenge to glorify God, it may first appear that God is supremely self-centered. But thoughtful reflection causes us to realize that to glorify God is for our best interest and great blessing. Our calling is to exhibit God's character. During his time on the earth, Jesus Christ was the perfect expression of God's character. He lived out the fruit of the Spirit: "...love, joy, peace, patience, kindness, goodness, faithfulness, gentleness and self-control." (Galatians 5:22). In human form Jesus was love in action and "Love is patient, love is kind. It does not envy, it does not boast, it is not proud. It is not rude, it is not self-seeking, it is not easily angered, it keeps no record of wrongs. Love does not delight in evil but rejoices with the truth. It always protects, always trusts, always hopes, always perseveres" (I Corinthians 13:4-7).

Just imagine how wonderful life would be if every Christian had "to glorify God" as his primary purpose. It would transform our personal lives, and all our relationships. It would certainly transform our churches. It would fulfill the command of Jesus: "Let your light so shine before men, that they may see your good works, and glorify your Father which is in heaven" (Matthew 5:16 KJV).

One aspect of God's character that is often overlooked is his compassion for the poor and persons with special needs.

Zechariah 7:10 reflects similar statements repeated in the Old Testament: "Do not oppress the widow or the fatherless, the alien or the poor... " In Deuteronomy alone, God's compassion for the "alien, the fatherless and the widow" is stated nine times.

Over and over again, the tests of leaders and of Israel were their devotion to God and their care for those on the margins of society. Religious observance, political power, military might and economic prosperity did not count for much if the needs of the widow, the fatherless, the foreigner and the poor were neglected.

A number of times Jesus referred to concern for the poor. An example is Luke 14:13:

"But when you give a banquet, invite the poor, the crippled, the lame, the blind... "

He describes his own ministry with these words:

"The Spirit of the Lord is on me, because he has anointed me to preach good news to the poor. He has sent me to proclaim freedom for the prisoners and recovery of sight for the blind, to release the oppressed, to proclaim the year of the Lord's favor" (Luke 4:18-19).

We are reminded in Hebrews 13:3 to "remember those in prison as if you were their fellow prisoners."

James declares:

"Religion that God our Father accepts as pure and faultless is this: to look after orphans and widows in their distress..." (James 1:27).

In many quarters of the evangelical church in America, this message has been neglected. There is a tendency to emphasize personal piety to the neglect of social compassion. The greatest number of the world's people is poor and needy. The church is called to be in the forefront of meeting their needs, nearby and in distant lands. Much is being done but much more needs to be done.

To Proclaim God's Message

The Greek word *euanggelizo* emphasizes the act of proclaiming. The Greek word *kerygma* denotes the content of the proclamation. C. H. Dodd has written a helpful summary of the content of **proclamation** *(kerygma)*.

First, the apostles declared that the messianic age had dawned.

"...this is what was spoken by the prophet Joel"
(Acts 2:16).

"But this is how God fulfilled what he had foretold through all the prophets..." (Acts 3:18).

"Indeed, all the prophets from Samuel on, as many as have spoken, have foretold these days" (Acts 3:24).

Second, the ministry, death, and resurrection of Jesus took place "...by God's set purpose and foreknowledge..." (Acts 2:23).

Third, because of the resurrection, Jesus has been exalted at the right hand of God as messianic head of the new Israel.

"Exalted to the right hand of God, he [Jesus] has received from the Father the promised Holy Spirit and has poured out what you now see and hear... Let all Israel be assured of this: God has made this Jesus... both Lord and Christ" (Acts 2:33-36).

"The God of Abraham, Isaac and Jacob, the God of our fathers, has glorified his servant Jesus" (Acts 3:13).

Fourth, the Holy Spirit in the church is the sign of Christ's present power and glory.

"...He [Jesus] has received from the Father the promised Holy Spirit and has poured out what you now see and hear" (Acts 2:33).

Fifth, the messianic age will reach its consummation when Christ returns.

"He must remain in heaven until the time comes for God to restore everything, as he promised long ago through his holy prophets" (Acts 3:21).

Finally, the *kerygma* always closes with an appeal for repentance, the offer of forgiveness and of the Holy Spirit, and the promise of "salvation," that is, "of the life of the Age to Come" to those who enter the elect community.

"Repent, and be baptized, every one of you, in the name of Jesus Christ for the forgiveness of your sins. And you will receive the gift of the Holy Spirit. The promise is for you and your children and for all who are far off – for all whom the Lord our God will call" (Acts 2:38-39).[113]

In current understanding, the word "proclaim" suggests preaching in a formal setting. However, the Greek word *euanggelizo* literally means "to announce news." It refers to a personal, one-to-one, setting as well as to a more public context. Luke tells us in Acts 8:4 "…those who had been scattered went about preaching [*euanggelizo*] the word" (NASB). These were ordinary Christians sharing the Gospel.

Philip is our example in preaching the Gospel in unevangelized areas. "Philip went down to the city of Samaria and proclaimed the Christ there" (Acts 8:5). He employed both public and private evangelism. "But when they believed Philip as he preached the good news of the Kingdom of God and the name of Jesus Christ, they were baptized, both men and women" (Acts 8:35). Privately, he witnessed to the Ethiopian eunuch (Acts 8:27-38).

Acts 8 stresses the role of the Holy Spirit in the Christian life. Jesus expressed his strong disapproval of the religious leaders of his day: "You are in error because you do not know the Scriptures or the power of God" (Matthew 22:29). In contrast, the early Christians knew and experienced both. As a result, "the Lord added to their number daily those who were being saved" (Acts 2:47).

To Disciple Believers

Jesus commands us to

"Go into all the world and preach the good news to all creation" (Mark 16:15).

Further, we are commissioned to

"…go and make disciples of all nations, baptizing them in the name of the Father and of the Son and of the Holy Spirit, and teaching them to obey everything I have commanded you. And surely I am with you always, to the very end of the age" (Matthew 28:19-20).

Discipleship can be defined as "to win another person to Christ and then take that person from the time of his conversion and help him become a solid, dedicated, committed, fruitful, mature disciple who could in time repeat that process in the life of another."[114]

The previous quote from Leroy Eims refers to one-on-one discipleship, but the more common pattern in the New Testament included discipling more than one at a time. Jesus discipled his Twelve, and gave special attention to Peter, James and John. Paul discipled not only his traveling companions, but also Timothy and pastors of other churches.

Though this text will not address discipleship methodology, it is necessary to point out some discipleship principles gleaned from the ministries of Jesus and the Apostle Paul.

1. The power of **personal example**: Robert Coleman says of Jesus, "He did not ask anyone to do or be anything which first He had not demonstrated in His own life."[115]

The Apostle Paul could say,

"Whatever you have learned or received or heard from me, or seen in me – put it into practice. And the God of peace will be with you" (Philippians 4:9).

May we all live in such a way that we can say the same!

2. The power of **association**: Without neglecting the larger ministry, Jesus concentrated his energy and ministry in only twelve "…that they might be *with* him…" (Mark 3:14).

Jesus modeled the importance of spending quality time with those being discipled.

3. The power of **delegation**: Mark 3:14 also shows that Jesus' desire was not to control, but to release – "that he might send them out to preach."

Our purpose is not to make our own disciples but to develop followers of Jesus.

4. The power of **instruction**:

"Now when he saw the crowds, he went up on a mountainside and sat down. His disciples came to him and he began to teach them…" (Matthew 5:1-2).

Jesus took his disciples aside and taught them. Some scholars think the "Sermon on the Mount" compiled by Matthew was based on a series of Jesus' teachings. John recorded Jesus' words at the Last Supper (chapters 13-14) and his discourse on the way to Gethsemane (chapters 15-16). Jesus constantly taught his disciples.

5. The power of **practical application**: Like Jesus, Paul dealt with real life, not just with theory. He reminded the new believers at Thessalonica, "...we instructed you *how* to live in order to please God" (I Thessalonians 4:1).

6. The power of **prayer**: Jesus' life was one of prayer. Certainly he prayed often for his disciples. His prayer life motivated them to request "teach us to pray" (Luke 11:1).

7. The power of **accountability**: The disciples reported back to Jesus after their ministry.

"The apostles gathered around Jesus and reported to him all they had done and taught" (Mark 6:30).

Objectives of Discipleship

The objectives of making disciples can be expressed in various ways. The Apostle Paul wrote,

"So, naturally, we proclaim Christ! We warn everyone we meet, and we teach everyone we can, all that we know about Him, so that, if possible, we may bring every man up to his full maturity in Jesus Christ. This is what I am working at all the time, with all the strength that God gives me" (Colossians 1:28-29, Phillips).

Paul encouraged Timothy to find reliable believers whom he could disciple.

"And the things you have heard me say in the presence of many witnesses entrust to reliable men who will also be qualified to teach others" (2 Timothy 2:2).

The ultimate objective of making disciples is to be obedient to our Lord's commission, "Make disciples of all nations." The

New Testament believers went out with the assurance of the presence and power of Jesus.

On the night of his betrayal, Jesus promised,

"The Spirit of truth... will be in you" (John 14:17).

Just before Jesus gave what we call the Great Commission he said,

"All authority in heaven and earth has been given to me" (Matthew 28:18).

At the conclusion of the commission he promised,

"...And surely I am with you always, to the very end of the age" (Matthew 28:20).

We have the incredible privilege of partnering with the Holy Spirit in disciple-making. So we can say, "Disciple making is a threefold relationship between the discipler, the disciple and the Holy Spirit. We can disciple with confidence when we are aware of the already present action of the Holy Spirit in the disciple's life."[116]

Biblical discipleship is not just behavior modification; it is character transformation as the Holy Spirit is released to do his work of forming Christ in the believer. This is often called "spiritual formation."

A church made up of true disciples will eagerly fulfill the Lord's Great Commission. It will be a part of a church planting movement because life produces life.

To limit the words of Jesus to discipling individuals is to do far less than he intended. We are to disciple nations.

"...go and make disciples of all nations..." (Matthew 28:19).

"This is done by ordinary Christians fulfilling God's calling to reform culture within their local spheres of influence – their families, churches, schools, neighborhoods, workplaces, professional organizations, and civic institutions."[117]

Who we are (witness), what we say (proclamation), and what we do (service) belong together in the mission of the church.

CHAPTER 2

THE SUFFERING OF THE CHURCH

New Testament Christians suffered. In a hostile world many Christians still suffer because of their faith. To assume otherwise is what Francis Schaeffer calls *utopianism*. According to some experts, today Christians worldwide experience more severe persecution than at any time in recent centuries.

Even in "Christian" America, believers face persecution. For instance, I personally know of two university professors whose biblical convictions cost them their jobs. A friend, who also teaches at a university, affirmed Christianity as a lifestyle in his classroom, then had to fight an extended legal battle to keep his job. In some U.S. cities, ordinances make it illegal for small groups to worship in private homes.

Admittedly, these restrictions pale compared to the rejection, torture, imprisonment and death believers around the world risk because of their faith in Jesus. Writing for a Western audience, Paul Scherer says, "To commit oneself to God is to make no detour around adversity... There is very little percentage to be had from playing about with Christianity on the theory that it is comfortable."[118]

According to the Apostle Peter, suffering for Christ's sake is to be expected. He also reminded his readers that such adversity results in a special blessing.

> "If you are insulted because of the name of Christ, you are blessed, for the spirit of glory and of God rests on you" (I Peter 4:14).

Paul, in referring to his own hardships, showed no bitterness.

"For our light and momentary troubles are achieving for us an eternal glory that far outweighs them all" (II Corinthians 4:17).

Later in the same epistle Paul gave details of his light afflictions (II Corinthians 6:4-10, 11:23-27), a harrowing list of calamities. Yet he arrived at a triumphant attitude towards them. Nowhere did he express resentment or question God. In fact, Paul actually rejoiced in suffering.

"...we also rejoice in our sufferings, because we know that suffering produces perseverance; perseverance, character; and character, hope. And hope does not disappoint us, because God has poured out his love into our hearts by the Holy Spirit, whom he has given us" (Romans 5:3-5).

James wrote,

"Consider it pure joy, my brothers, whenever you face trials of many kinds, because you know that the testing of your faith develops perseverance" (James 1:2-3).

The writer of Hebrews readily made the transition from the present suffering to the future bliss awaiting believers.

"Remember those earlier days after you had received the light, when you stood your ground in a great contest in the face of suffering. Sometimes you were publicly exposed to insult and persecution; at other times you stood side by side with those who were so treated. You sympathized with those in prison and joyfully accepted the confiscation of your property, because you knew that you yourselves had better and lasting possessions. So do not throw away your confidence; it will be richly rewarded. You need to persevere so that when you have done the will of God, you will receive what he has promised" (Hebrews 10:32-36).

I pray that God will give us such an attitude toward suffering for Christ.

"It cannot be said that the New Testament answers all the intellectual problems which arise from God's permitting human suffering, but it does enable Christians to face suffering without losing confidence in the perfection of God's wisdom."[119]

CHAPTER 3

THE LIVING HOPE OF THE CHURCH

The Apostle Peter declared,

"Praise be to the God and Father of our Lord Jesus Christ! In his great mercy he has given us new birth into a living hope through the resurrection of Jesus Christ from the dead, and into an inheritance that can never perish, spoil or fade – kept in heaven for you," (I Peter 1:3-4).

The Apostle Paul wrote of the "blessed hope," anchored in the redemptive work of Christ.

"...while we wait for the blessed hope – the glorious appearing of our great God and Savior, Jesus Christ, who gave himself for us to redeem us from all wickedness and to purify for himself a people that are his very own, eager to do what is good" (Titus 2:13-14).

From these passages and others we see that for the Early Church, the Second Coming of Christ was not some doctrine relegated to the distant future but a living reality that conditioned their daily lives. A product of this "blessed hope" is a people "eager to do what is good." Faith and love spring from this hope.

"We always thank God, the Father of our Lord Jesus Christ, when we pray for you, because we have heard of your faith in Christ Jesus and of the love you have for all the saints – the faith and love that spring from the hope that is stored up for you in heaven and that you have already heard about in the word of truth, the gospel that has come to you" (Colossians 1:3-5).

The Apostle John wrote,

"How great is the love the Father has lavished on us, that we should be called children of God! And that is what we are! The reason the world does not know us is that it did not know him. Dear friends, now we are children of God, and what we will be has not yet been made known. But we know that when he appears, we shall be like him, for we shall see him as he is. Everyone who has this hope in him purifies himself, just as he is pure" (I John 3:1-3).

The Bible is not a book of theory; it is a book of practice, and every doctrine of the New Testament has immediate application to everyday life. "The entire New Testament is eschatological in that it sees history as being moved under God toward a goal... Only Philemon (25 verses) and 3 John (15 verses) are without reference to hopes and expectations concerning the future and the last things."[120]

R. J. Bauckham asserts, "The biblical writings understand history as a linear movement towards a goal. God is driving history towards the ultimate fulfillment of his purposes for his creation. So biblical eschatology is not limited to the destiny of the individual; it concerns the consummation of the whole history of the world, towards which all God's redemptive acts in history are directed."[121]

New Testament writers often referred to "end time" events. Their words have been interpreted in many ways, causing conflicting opinions concerning the "signs of the times" – the tribulation, the thousand years referred to in Daniel and Revelation, to mention just two. Certain events, however, are indisputable.[122]

1.   The same Jesus of Nazareth who ascended into heaven will personally come back to earth.

"...this same Jesus, who has been taken from you into heaven, will come back in the same way you have seen him go into heaven" (Acts 1:11).

2. Everyone on earth will know of his coming.

"Look, he is coming with the clouds, and every eye will see him, even those who pierced him..." (Revelation 1:7).

3. He will come in power and glory.

"...They will see the Son of Man coming on the clouds of the sky, with power and great glory" (Matthew 24:30).

4. He will destroy Antichrist.

"And then the lawless one will be revealed, whom the Lord Jesus will overthrow with the breath of his mouth and destroy by the splendor of his coming" (II Thessalonians 2:8).

5. He will gather his people, living and dead.

"For the Lord himself will come down from heaven, with a loud command, with the voice of the archangel and with the trumpet call of God, and the dead in Christ will rise first. After that, we who are still alive and are left will be caught up together with them in the clouds to meet the Lord in the air. And so we will be with the Lord forever" (I Thessalonians 4:16-17).

6. He will judge the world.

It is generally understood that two final judgments are mentioned in the New Testament.

One is the Judgment Seat of Christ (Bema Seat) for believers in reference to rewards or lack thereof.

"For we must all appear before the judgment seat of Christ, that each one may receive what is due him for the things done while in the body, whether good or bad" (II Corinthians 5:10).

The other is the Great White Throne Judgment for unbelievers who will be eternally separated from God.

"Then I saw a great white throne and him who was seated on it... And I saw the dead, great and small, standing before the throne, and books were opened... If anyone's name was not found in the book of life, he was thrown into the lake of fire" (Revelation 20:11-15).

Our Blessed Hope

The New Testament declares that in eternity the believer will be **with** Christ, **like** Christ, and will **co-reign** with him. We will be gathered around the Throne of God with a great multitude that no one can count from every nation, tribe, people and language.

"After this I looked and there before me was a great multitude that no one could count, from every nation, tribe, people and language, standing before the throne and in front of the Lamb... And they cried out in a loud voice: 'Salvation belongs to our God, who sits on the throne, and to the Lamb'" (Revelation. 7:9-10).

"Then I saw a new heaven and a new earth, for the first heaven and the first earth had passed away, and there was no longer any sea. I saw the Holy City, the new Jerusalem, coming down out of heaven from God, prepared as a bride beautifully dressed for her husband. And I heard a loud voice from the throne saying, 'Now the dwelling of God is with men, and he will live with them. They will be his people, and God himself will be with them and be their God. He will wipe every tear from their eyes. There will be no more death or mourning or crying or pain, for the old order of things has passed away'" (Revelation 21:1-4).

CONCLUSION

An excerpt from a paper prepared for an international conference held at Northwestern University in 1954 provides an appropriate conclusion to this book.

"To those who ask, 'What will happen to the world?' we answer, 'His kingdom is coming.' To those who ask, 'What is before us?' we answer, 'He, the King, stands before us.' To those who ask, 'What may we expect?' we answer, 'We are not standing before a pathless wilderness of unfulfilled time, with a goal which no one would dare to predict; we are gazing upon our living Lord, our Judge and Savior, who was dead and lives forevermore; upon the one who has come and is coming, and who will reign for ever. It may be that we shall encounter affliction; yes, that must be if we want to participate in him. But we know his word, his royal word: 'Be comforted, I have overcome the world.'"[123]

APPENDICES

APPENDIX 1

THE CHARACTER OF GOD

Upon reading the Old Testament, we may think of God as harsh and unyielding. We get a different impression when reading Exodus 33 and 34:

"Then Moses said, 'Now show me your glory.' And the Lord said, 'I will cause all my goodness to pass in front of you, and I will proclaim my name, the Lord, in your presence. I will have mercy on whom I will have mercy, and I will have compassion on whom I will have compassion. But,' he said, 'you cannot see my face, for no one may see me and live.'

Then the Lord said, 'There is a place near me where you may stand on a rock. When my glory passes by, I will put you in a cleft in the rock and cover you with my hand until I have passed by. Then I will remove my hand and you will see my back; but my face must not be seen'" (Exodus 33:18-23).

"Then the Lord came down in the cloud and stood there with him and proclaimed his name, the Lord. And he passed in front of Moses, proclaiming, 'The Lord, the Lord, the compassionate and gracious God, slow to anger, abounding in love and faithfulness, maintaining love to thousands, and forgiving wickedness, rebellion and sin. Yet he does not leave the guilty unpunished; he punishes the children and their children for the sin of the fathers to the third and fourth generation'" (Exodus 34:5-7).

The same statement, with various wordings, appears throughout the Old Testament. Some examples are Numbers 14:18-19, Nehemiah 9:17, Psalm 86:15, Psalm 103:8, Psalm 145:8, Joel 2:13 and Jonah 4:2.

Moses' immediate response to this revelation was to bow to the ground and worship (Exodus 34:8).

Regarding the generational curse pronounced in Exodus 34:7 and in some of the other passages cited, many believers do not know that such a curse can be broken.

"Christ redeemed us from the curse of the law by becoming a curse for us, for it is written: 'Cursed is everyone who is hung on a tree.' He redeemed us in order that the blessing given to Abraham might come to the Gentiles through Christ Jesus, so that by faith we might receive the promise of the Spirit" (Galatians 3:13-14).

In the name of Jesus, a believer can declare that a generational curse is no longer in effect. In Christ we can claim God's promise of Exodus 20:6, "showing love to a thousand generations of those who love me and keep my commandments."

The names for God found in the Old Testament tell us much about who he is and what he does. A partial list of the Hebrew names of God follows.

EL SHADDAI – (Genesis 17:1) God almighty, all powerful, all sufficient
ADONAI – (Genesis 15:2) the Lord and Master
JEHOVAH-JIREH – (Genesis 22:14) the Lord will provide
JEHOVAH-RAPHA – (Exodus 15:26) the Lord who heals
JEHOVAH-NISSI – (Exodus 17:15) the Lord my banner (of victory)
JEHOVAH-MEKODDISHKEM – (Exodus 31:13) the Lord who sanctifies you or the Lord who makes you holy
JEHOVAH-SHALOM – (Judges 6:24) the Lord is peace
JEHOVAH-RAAH - (Psalm 23:1) the Lord my shepherd
JEHOVAH-TSIDKENU – (Jeremiah 23:6) the Lord our righteousness
JEHOVAH-SHAMMAH – (Ezekiel 48:35) the Lord is there (present).

For an excellent study on the names of God, see Kay Arthur's book *Lord, I Want to Know You* published by Fleming H. Revell.

The prophet Isaiah ascribes other names to God in reference to the Messiah:

"For to us a child is born, to us a son is given, and the government will be on his shoulders. And he will be called Wonderful Counselor, Mighty God, Everlasting Father, Prince of Peace" (Isaiah 9:6).

In the words of the psalmist:

"Those who know your name will trust in you, for you, Lord, have never forsaken those who seek you" (Psalm 9:10).

APPENDIX 2

"ONE ANOTHER" SCRIPTURES

We are to LOVE one another.

John 13:34-35	I Thessalonians 3:12	Hebrews 10:24
John 15:12,17	I Thessalonians 4:9	I Peter 1:22

I John 3:11, 23
I John. 4:7, 11, 12

We are to yield to others, serving their interests.

BE DEVOTED	BE HUMBLE	SUBMIT
Romans 12:10	I Peter 5:5	Ephesians 5:21
		I Peter 5:5

SERVE
Galatians 5:13
Hebrews 10:24

We are to spend time with one another.

GREET	BE HOSPITABLE	HAVE FELLOWSHIP
Romans 16:16	I Peter 4:9	I John 1:7
I Corinthians 16:20		
II Corinthians 13:12		
I Peter 5:14		

We are to allow others to be imperfect.

BE PATIENT	ACCEPT	BEAR WITH
Ephesians 4:2	Romans 15:7	Galatians 6:2
Colossians 3:13		Colossians 3:13

BE AT PEACE	WAIT FOR	FORGIVE
Mark 9:50	I Corinthians 11:33	Ephesians 4:32
		Colossians 3:13

Our words should build up and be helpful to one another.

BUILD UP	SPEAK TRUTH	ADMONISH
Romans 14:19	Ephesians 4:25	Romans 15:14
I Thessalonians 5:11	Colossians 3:9	Colossians 3:16
Hebrews 3:13		Hebrews 10:24-25

CONFESS	PRAY
James 5:16	James 5:16

We are to have a gentle heart toward others in difficulty.

CARE FOR	COMFORT	BE KIND
I Corinthians 12:25	I Thessalonians 4:18	Ephesians 4:32

BE COMPASSIONATE
I Peter 3:8

We are to be in unity with one another.

SAME MIND	MEMBERS
II Corinthians 13:11	Romans 12:5
Acts 4:32	Romans 15:5

APPENDIX 3

A PARTIAL LIST OF SINS REQUIRING CHURCH DISCIPLINE

1. Sexual immorality

    a. fornication, *i.e.*, voluntary sexual intercourse between two persons not married to each other (Mark 7:21)

    b. adultery, *i.e.*, voluntary sexual intercourse between a married person with someone other than his/her marriage partner (Mark 7:21)

    c. homosexuality and lesbianism, *i.e.*, sexual relations with a person of the same sex (Romans 1:26-27)

    d. lewdness, *i.e.*, "eagerness for lustful pleasure" (NLT), which may include pornography, child molestation or voyeurism (Mark 7:22)

2. Fits of rage, "outbursts of anger" (NLT), in any context but particularly in the family where anger often results in physical abuse (Galatians 5:20)

3. Drunkenness (Galatians 5:21)

4. Orgies, "participating in wild parties" (NLT), (Galatians 5:21)

5. Witchcraft, "participating in demonic activities" (NLT), (Galatians 5:20)

6. Theft (Mark 7:21)

7. Slander, *i.e.*, malicious misrepresentation of another person with the resulting damage to his/her reputation (Mark 7:22)

8. "those who cause divisions" either by words or actions (Romans 16:17; Titus 3:10)

9. Advocating or teaching the rejection of the essential biblical doctrines, *i.e.* heresy, (I Timothy 6:3-5; I John 4:1-3; II John 7-11)

NOTE: Every effort should be patiently made to restore to wholeness persons with addictions and confused sexual orientation.

APPENDIX 4

ADDITIONAL RESOURCES

BOOKS

Brock, Charles, *The Principles and Practice of Indigenous Church Planting*. Nashville:Broadman Press, 1981.

Comiskey, Joel T., *Home Cell Group Explosion: How Your Small Group Can Grow and Multiply*. Houston: Touch Publications, 1998.

Garrison, David, *Church Planting Movements: How God is Redeeming a Lost World*. Midlothian: WIGTake Resources, 2004.

Greeson, Kevin, *Camel Training Manual*. Midlothian: WIGTake Resources, 2004.

Hadaway, C. Kirk, Wright, Stuart A., DuBose, Francis M., *Home Cell Groups and House Churches*. Nashville: Broadman Press, 1987.

Neighbour, Ralph W., Jr. *The Shepherd's Guidebook*. Houston: Touch Publications, 1992.

Neighbour, Ralph W., Jr. *Where Do We Go from Here?: A Guidebook for the Cell Group Church* (Tenth Anniversary Edition). Houston: Touch Publications, 2000.

Overman, Christiann, *Assumptions that Affect our Lives*. Charleston Group, 1996.

Patterson, George, *Church Multiplication Guide*. William Carey Library Pub., Revised edition, 2003.

WEB SITES

Dawn Ministries, www.dawnministries.org

House Church Central, www.hccentral.com

House 2 House, www.house2house.tv/

Mentorlink International, www.mentorlink.org

Touch Family Church (Dr. Ralph Neighbour), www.touchfamily.com

Touch Ministries, www.touchusa.org

Among the resources offered on this web site are books and articles relating to ministry to children in the cell church context. Look for authors Lorna Jenkins and Daphne Kirk.

WORKS CITED

Allen, Charles L. *God's Psychiatry*. Old Tappan: Fleming H. Revell, 1953.

Anderson, Keith R. and Randy Reese. *Spiritual Mentoring*. Downers Grove: InterVarsity, 1999.

Anderson, Neil. *Victory over the Darkness*. Ventura: Regal Books, 1990.

Baker, J. P. "Prophecy, Prophets." *New Bible Dictionary*. Edited by J. D. Douglas and N. Hillyer. 2nd ed. Wheaton: Tyndale House, 1982: 975-986.

Bauckham, R. J. "Eschatology." *New Bible Dictionary*. Edited by J. D. Douglas and N. Hillyer. 2nd. ed. Wheaton: Tyndale House, 1982: 342-348.

Bray, Gerald. *The Doctrine of God*. Downers Grove: InterVarsity, 1993.

Bugbee, Bruce. *What You Do Best in the Body of Christ*. Grand Rapids: Zondervan, 1995.

Buttrick, George A. *Prayer*. Nashville: Abingdon, 1942.

Cerling, Charles E., Jr. "Forgiveness Is Not a One-Shot Deal." *Eternity Magazine* (June, 1980): 30.

Chambers, Oswald. *My Utmost For His Highest*. Edited by James Reimann. Grand Rapids: Discovery House, 1992.

Christenson, Larry. *A Message to the Charismatic Movement*. Minneapolis: Dimension Books, 1972.

Coleman, Robert E. *The Master Plan of Evangelism*. Old Tappan: Fleming H. Revell, 1963.

Cooke, Jerry. *Love, Acceptance and Forgiveness*. Glendale: G/L Regal Books, 1979.

Dodd, C. H. *Apostolic Preaching*. New York and London: Harper & Brothers, 1960.

Eims, Leroy. *The Lost Art of Disciple Making*. Grand Rapids: Zondervan, 1978.

Fischer, John. *On a Hill Too Far Away*. Ann Arbor: Servant Publications, 1994.

Foster, Richard. *Prayer*. San Francisco: Harper Collins, 1992.

George, Timothy. "Big Picture of Faith." *Christianity Today* (October 23, 2000): 90.

George, Timothy. *Theology of the Reformers*. Nashville: Broadman and Holman, 1988.

Gill, John. *Expositions of the Old and New Testaments*. Grand Rapids: Baker, 1982. Volume 5, Matthew-Acts.

Grudem, Wayne. *Systematic Theology*. Grand Rapids: Zondervan, 1994.

Guthrie, Donald. *New Testament Theology*. Downers Grove: InterVarsity, 1981.

Guthrie, Stan. "The Evangelical Scandal," *Christianity Today* (April, 2005): 70-73.

Harkness, Georgia. *Prayer and the Common Life*. New York: Abingdon-Cokesbury, 1948.

Hart, Larry A. *Truth Aflame*. Nashville: Thomas Nelson, 1999.

Hays, Richard B. *The Moral Vision of the New Testament*. San Francisco: HarperSanFrancisco, 1996.

Jones, Gregory. *Embodying Forgiveness, A Theological Analysis*. Grand Rapids: Eerdmans, 1995.

Laney, J. Carl. *A Guide to Church Discipline*. Minneapolis: Bethany House, 1985.

Lewis, C. S. *Mere Christianity*. New York: MacMillan, 1960.

Lloyd-Jones, D. Martyn. *Studies in the Sermon on the Mount*. Grand Rapids: Eerdmans, 1972.

Lochman, Jan M. *Living Roots of Reformation*. Minneapolis: Augsburg, 1979.

MacDonald, Gordon. *Restoring Your Spiritual Passion*. Nashville: Oliver-Nelson Books, 1986.

McGee, Robert S. *The Search for Significance*. Houston: Rapha, 1987.

McMillen, S. I., M. D. *None of These Diseases*. Revised and updated by David E. Stern. Grand Rapids: Fleming H. Revell, 1984.

Manning, Brennan. *Reflections for Ragamuffins*. San Francisco: Harper, 1997.

Maxwell, L. E. *Born Crucified*. Chicago: Moody, 1953.

Morris, L. L. "Forgiveness." *New Bible Dictionary*. Edited by J. D. Douglas and N. Hillyer. 2nd ed. Wheaton: Tyndale House, 1982: 390-391.

Myers, Ruth. *31 Days of Praise*. Singapore: The Navigators, 1992.

Olford, Stephen. *The Grace of Giving*. Grand Rapids: Baker Book House, 1972.

Packer, J. I. "Experiencing God's Presents." *Christianity Today* (August, 2003): 55.

Packer, J. I. *Knowing God*. Downers Grove: InterVarsity, 1973.

Packer, J. I. "Incarnation." *New Bible Dictionary*. Edited by J. D. Douglas and N. Hillyer. 2nd. ed. Wheaton: Tyndale House, 1982: 510-513.

Pearcey, Nancy. *Total Truth, Liberating Christianity from its Cultural Captivity*. Wheaton: Crossway Books, 2004.

Redpath, Alan. *Victorious Praying*. Old Tappan: Fleming H. Revell, 1957.

Scherer, Paul. *Love is a Spendthrift*. New York: Harper & Brothers, 1961.

Schaeffer, Francis A. *Genesis in space and time*. Downers Grove: InterVarsity Press, 1972.

Sherman, Dean. *Spiritual Warfare for Every Christian*. Seattle: YWAM Publishing, 1990.

Smedes, Lewis B. "Forgiveness: The Power to Change the Past." *Christianity Today* (January 7, 1983): 22-26.

Snyder, Howard A. *The Community of the King*. Downers Grove: InterVarsity, 1977.

Snyder, Howard A. *The Problem of Wineskins*. Downers Grove: InterVarsity, 1976.

Stackhouse, John G., Jr. "Mind Over Skepticism." *Christianity Today* (June 11, 2001): 74.

Stagg, Frank. *The Book of Acts*. Nashville: Broadman, 1955.

Stagg, Frank. *New Testament Theology*. Nashville: Baptist Sunday School Board, 1962.

Stedman, Ray C. *Body Life*. Glendale: G/L Regal Books, 1972.

Stott, John R. W. *Christian Counter-Culture*. Downers Grove: InterVarsity, 1979.

Stott, John R. W. *The Cross of Christ*. Downers Grove: InterVarsity, 1986.

Strong, A. H. *Systematic Theology*. Philadelphia: Judson, 1953.

Tenny, Merril C. "The Gospel of John." *The Expositor's Bible Commentary*. Edited by Frank E. Gaebelein. Vol. 9. Grand Rapids: Zondervan, 1981: 29.

Thompson, Bruce. *Walls of My Heart*. Euclid: Crown Ministries International, 1989.

Tozier, *The Best of A. W. Tozier*. Compiled by Warren Wiersbe. Harrisburg: Christian Publications, 1978.

Trench, Richard. *Synonyms of the New Testament*. Grand Rapids: Eerdmans, 1948.

Wallis, Arthur. *God's Chosen Fast*. Fort Washington: Christian Literature Crusade, 1986.

NOTES

1 Gerald Bray, *The Doctrine of God* (Downers Grove: InterVarsity, 1993), 51.

2 Oswald Chambers, *My Utmost For His Highest*, ed. James Reimann (Grand Rapids:Discovery House,1992), July 27.

3 *The Best of A. W. Tozier*, compiled by Warren Wiersbe (Harrisburg: Christian Publications, 1978), 21.

4 Nancy R. Pearcey, *Total Truth, Liberating Christianity from its Cultural Captivity* (Wheaton: Crossway Books, 2004), 47.

5 Francis A. Schaeffer, *Genesis in space and time,*(Downers Grove: InterVarsity Press,1972), 72.

6 Dean Sherman, *Spiritual Warfare for Every Christian* (Seattle: YWAM Publishing, 1990), Chapter 9.

7 Neil Anderson, *Victory Over the Darkness* (Ventura: Regal Books, 1990), 170.

8 Richard B. Hays, *The Moral Vision of the New Testament* (San Francisco: HarperSanFrancisco, 1996), 296.

9 Beeson Divinity School of Samford University, Birmingham, Alabama.

10 Merril C. Tenny, "The Gospel of John," *The Expositor's Bible Commentary*, ed. Frank E. Gaebelein. Vol. 9 (Grand Rapids: Zondervan, 1981), 29.

11 J. I. Packer, "Incarnation," *New Bible Dictionary*, Ed. J.D. Douglas and N. Hillyer, Second Edition (Wheaton: Tyndale House, 1982), 510-513.

12 Brennan Manning, *Reflections for Ragamuffins* (San Francisco: Harper, 1997), August 2.

13 George A. Buttrick, *Prayer* (Nashville: Abingdon, 1942), 29.

14 John Fischer, *On a Hill Too Far Away* (Ann Arbor: Servant Publications, 1994), 15-17, 33-34.

15 Chambers, April 6.

16 An old Latin proverb.

17 John R. W. Stott, *The Cross of Christ* (Downers Grove: InterVarsity, 1986), 190.

18 Stott, *The Cross*, 160.

[19] Stott, quoting E. Brunner, *The Cross*, 201.

[20] Robert S. McGee, *The Search For Significance*, (Houston: Rapha, 1987),43.

[21] Stott, *The Cross*, 105, 173.

[22] Paul Scherer, *Love is a Spendthrift* (New York: Harper & Brothers, 1961), 158.

[23] Scherer, 49.

[24] Stott, *The Cross,*193.

[25] Neil Anderson, 56.

[26] I recommend L. E. Maxwell's book *Born Crucified* (Chicago: Moody, 1953), an excellent treatment of this truth.

[27] Chambers, Oct. 5.

[28] C. S. Lewis, *Mere Christianity*, (New York: MacMillan, 1960), 167.

[29] Stott, *The Cross*, 282.

[30]* Fischer, 126.

[31] Donald Guthrie, *New Testament Theology* (Downers Grove: InterVarsity, 1981), 377.

[32] Hays, 46.

[33] Gregory Jones, *Embodying Forgiveness, A Theological Analysis* (Grand Rapids: Eerdmans, 1995), 124.

[34] I'm indebted to my friend, Ben Loring, for these observations about the difference between the church and the kingdom.

[35] Guthrie, 788.

[36] Howard A. Snyder, quoting Elton Trueblood, *The Problem of Wineskins* (Downers Grove: InterVarsity, 1976), 141.

[37] Snyder, *Problem of Wineskins*, 139-140.

[38] Used by permission

[39] A. H. Strong, *Systematic Theology*, Seventeenth Printing (Philadelphia: Judson, 1953), 263.

[40] Timothy George, "Big Picture of Faith," *Christianity Today,* October 23, 2000, 90.

[41] Strong, 268.

[42] Strong, 291.

[43] Strong, 292.

[44] Chambers, July 29.

[45] Frank Stagg, *The Book of Acts* (Nashville: Broadman, 1955), 67.

[46] Jones, 119.

[47] Stagg, quoting John Macmurray, *Book of Acts*, 67-69.

[48] Jerry Cook, *Love, Acceptance and Forgiveness* (Glendale: G/L Regal Books,1979), 13.

[49] Chambers, May 3.

[50] Jones, 45-46.

[51] S. I. McMillen, M.D., *None of These Diseases*, revised and updated by David E. Stern (Old Tappan: Fleming H. Revell, 1984), 108.

[52] Gordon MacDonald, *Restoring Your Spiritual Passion* (Nashville: Oliver-Nelson Books, 1986), 105.

[53] L. L. Morris, "Forgiveness," *New Bible Dictionary*, Editors: J.D. Douglas and N. Hillyer, Second Edition (Wheaton: Tyndale House, 1982), 391.

[54] Bruce Thompson, *Walls of My Heart* (Euclid: Crown Ministries International,1989), 201.

[55] Jones, 162, 218.

[56] *Ibid.*, 148.

[57] *Ibid.*, 113.

[58] Charles E. Cerling, Jr, "Forgiveness Is Not a One-Shot Deal," *Eternity Magazine*, June 1980, 30.

[59] Lewis B. Smedes, "Forgiveness: The Power to Change the Past," *Christianity Today*, January 7, 1983, 22.

[60] Jones, quoting Jon Sobrino, 63.

[61] Stephen Olford, *The Grace of Giving* (Grand Rapids, Baker, 1972), 37-38.

[62] I am indebted to my wife, Frances, for the format presented here.

[63] J. I. Packer, *Knowing God* (Downers Grove: InterVarsity, 1973), 182.

[64] Stott, *The Cross*, 146.

[65] Alan Redpath, *Victorious Praying* (Old Tappan: Fleming H. Revell, 1957), 18.

[66] Stott, *The Cross,* 147.

[67] Georgia Harkness, *Prayer and the Common Life* (New York: Abingdon-Cokesbury, 1948), 27, 38.

[68] Redpath, 18.

[69] Richard Foster, *Prayer* (San Francisco: Harper Collins, 1992), 191.

[70] Charles L. Allen, *God's Psychiatry* (Old Tappan: Fleming H. Revell, 1953), 111.

[71] Chambers, February 18.

[72] Manning, quoting Francis Macnutt, August 28.

[73] D. Martyn Lloyd-Jones, *Studies in the Sermon on the Mount* (Grand Rapids: Eerdmans, 1972), 37.

[74] Roy Lessin, from a Day Spring greeting card.

[75] See the discussion of forgiveness in "Fellowship *(Koinonia),*" Part Two, Chapter Two.

[76] Redpath, 85.

[77] I am indebted to Dr. A. T. Robertson for the insights in this paragraph.

[78] Ruth Myers, *31 Days of Praise* (Singapore, The Navigators, 1992), Day 26.

[79] John Gill, *Expositions of the Old and New Testaments,* Volume 5, Matthew-Acts (Grand Rapids: Baker, 1982), Gill's observations on Matthew 6:13 quoting Seder Tephillot, edited by Basil, fol. 280.1.

[80] *Ibid.* fol. 70.2.

[81] John R. W. Stott, *Christian Counter-Culture* (Downers Grove: InterVarsity, 1979), 135.

[82] *Ibid.,* 138.

[83] Arthur Wallis, *God's Chosen Fast* (Fort Washington: Christian Literature Crusade, 1986), Selected from extensive lists in the book.

[84] Stott, *Christian Counter Culture,* 137.

[85] T. C. Smith, classroom lecture, Southern Baptist Seminary, 1954.

[86] Jones, 167.

[87] Timothy George, *Theology of the Reformers* (Nashville: Broadman and Holman, 1988), 319.

[88] *Ibid.,* 319-320.

[89] Frank Stagg, *New Testament Theology* (Nashville: Baptist Sunday School Board, 1962), 273.

[90] J. Carl Laney, *A Guide to Church Discipline* (Minneapolis: Bethany House, 1985), 11.

[91] *Ibid.,* Quoted by Laney, 44.

[92] Stan Guthrie, quoting Ron Sider, "The Evangelical Scandal," *Christianity Today*, April, 2005, 70-73.

[93] Jones, 270.

[94] Jones, 270.

[95] Larry A. Hart, *Truth Aflame* (Nashville: Thomas Nelson, 1999), 513.

[96] J. I. Packer, "Experiencing God's Presents," *Christianity Today*, August, 2003, 55.

[97] Wayne Grudem, *Systematic Theology* (Grand Rapids: Zondervan, 1994), 1049.

[98] Jack Hayford, Lecture at Pastor's Conference, Church On the Way, Van Nuys, CA, 1987.

[99] Bruce Bugbee, *What You Do Best in the Body of Christ* (Grand Rapids: Zondervan, 1995).

[100] Bugbee, 70.

[101] Bugbee, 73.

[102] J. I. Packer, "Experiencing God's Presents," *Christianity Today*, August, 2003, 55.

[103] Larry Christenson, *A Message to the Charismatic Movement* (Minneapolis: Dimension Books, 1972), 66.

[104] See note 98.

[105] Christenson, 63.

[106] Chambers, May 6.

[107] Howard A. Snyder, *The Community of the King* (Downers Grove: InterVarsity, 1977), 87-88.

[108] Ray C. Stedman, *Body Life* (Glendale: G/L Regal Books, 1972), 72.

[109] Richard Trench, *Synonyms of the New Testament* (Grand Rapids: Eerdmans, 1948), 21.

[110] J. P. Baker, "Prophecy, Prophets," *New Bible Dictionary*, Editors: J.D. Douglas and N. Hillyer, Second Edition (Wheaton: Tyndale House, 1982), 984.

[111] The metaphor of motor and steering wheel is not original with me, but I cannot locate the source.

[112] Stedman, 15.

[113] C. H. Dodd, *Apostolic Preaching* (New York and London: Harper & Brothers, 1960), 21-23.

[114] Leroy Eims, *The Lost Art of Disciple Making* (Grand Rapids: Zondervan, 1978), 18.

[115] Robert E. Coleman, *The Master Plan of Evangelism* (Old Tappan: Fleming H. Revell, 1963), 80.

[116] Adapted from *Spiritual Mentoring*, Keith R. Anderson, Randy Reese (Downers Grove: InterVarsity, 1999), 12.

[117] Pearcey, *Total Truth*, 19.

[118] Scherer, 158.

[119] Guthrie, 99.

[120] Stagg, quoting H. A. Guy, *New Testament Theology*, 305.

[121] R. J.Bauckham, "Eschatology," *New Bible Dictionary*, Editors: J.D. Douglas and N. Hillyer, Second Edition (Wheaton: Tyndale House, 1982), 342.

[122] *Ibid.*, I owe the following arrangement of ideas to R. J.Bauckham.

[123] Jan M. Lochman quoting *"Christus, die Hoffnung fur die Welt"* (Christ the Hope of the World), *Living Roots of Reformation* (Minneapolis: Augsburg, 1979), 65.